Contents Guide

Section 5: Enhancing Quality with Test Plans and Extensions

Section 6: Continuous Monitoring and Optimization

~ Conclusion

Section 1:
Introduction to Azure DevOps

Welcome & What You'll Learn

Welcome to the World of Azure DevOps

Congratulations on embarking on your journey to master Azure DevOps! This book is your guide to transforming the way you develop and deliver software, enabling your teams to achieve new levels of speed, efficiency, and quality.

In today's fast-paced digital world, the ability to deliver software quickly and reliably is not just a competitive advantage – it's a necessity. With Azure DevOps, you'll gain access to a powerful suite of tools that will streamline your entire software development lifecycle (SDLC).

What is Azure DevOps?

At its core, Azure DevOps is a cloud-based platform from Microsoft that fosters collaboration between development and operations teams. It brings together a comprehensive set of services that help you:

- **Plan and Track Work:** Azure Boards provides agile tools to manage projects, track work items, and visualize progress.
- **Manage Code:** Azure Repos offers Git-based repositories for highly collaborative version control.
- **Build and Test:** Azure Pipelines empowers you to create robust continuous integration and continuous delivery (CI/CD) processes for automated building and testing of your code.
- **Deploy and Monitor:** Azure Pipelines also allows you to set up release pipelines to automate deployments to various environments and continuously monitor applications in production.

- **Extend and Integrate:** Azure DevOps offers a rich Marketplace and extensive APIs for customizing it with extensions and integrations, allowing it to fit seamlessly in your existing toolchain.

Why Learn Azure DevOps?

Here's why investing your time in mastering Azure DevOps is worthwhile:

- **Empower Collaboration:** DevOps breaks down the silos between development and operations, leading to smoother release cycles and faster problem resolution.
- **Reduce Time-to-Market:** Automated processes significantly accelerate releases, helping you quickly deliver features and updates to your users.
- **Elevate Code Quality:** Built-in testing and quality checks lead to fewer bugs, improving software reliability and customer satisfaction.
- **Streamline Workflows:** Integrated tools within Azure DevOps provide a seamless and consistent experience for your teams.
- **Embrace the Cloud:** Azure DevOps is inherently scalable and integrates with a vast range of other Azure services.

What You'll Gain from This Book

This book is your hands-on companion as you navigate the world of Azure DevOps. Through practical examples and step-by-step guides, you will:

- Set up and configure your Azure DevOps organization.
- Master how to use Azure Boards for flexible project management.
- Learn the ins and outs of Git version control with Azure Repos.
- Construct effective CI/CD pipelines to automate builds, tests, and deployments.
- Enhance your software quality through Azure Test Plans.
- Implement application monitoring and alerting with Application Insights.
- Optimize your DevOps processes and improve your team's effectiveness.

Getting Started

Before you dive into the following chapters, here's what you need:

- **A Microsoft account:** Visit https://www.microsoft.com/ to create one.
- **An Azure subscription:** If you don't have one, sign up for a free trial at https://azure.microsoft.com/.

Let's Get Rolling!

With Azure DevOps in your toolkit, you'll be equipped to supercharge your software development processes. So, get ready! Your journey to DevOps mastery begins now, and this book is your guide.

Additional Resources

- **Azure DevOps Documentation:** https://docs.microsoft.com/en-us/azure/devops/?view=azure-devops
- **Azure DevOps Blog:** https://devblogs.microsoft.com/devops/

Hands-On: Setting Up Your Azure DevOps Organization

Welcome to the practical part of your Azure DevOps adventure! In this chapter, you'll take your first steps and create your very own Azure DevOps organization. This organization will serve as the central hub for all your software development projects, so let's get it set up.

Prerequisites

- **A Microsoft Account:** If you don't have one already, head over to https://www.microsoft.com/ and create one for free.
- **An Azure Subscription:** A free Azure trial will work for this. If you don't have a subscription, sign up at https://azure.microsoft.com/.

Step-by-Step Guide

1. **Navigate to the Azure DevOps Portal:** Visit the Azure DevOps portal at https://dev.azure.com/.
2. **Sign Up:** Click on the "Start free" button.
3. **Authenticate with your Microsoft Account:** Sign in with the Microsoft account you created or wish to associate with your Azure DevOps organization.
4. **Choose a Name:** Enter a unique name for your Azure DevOps organization. This name forms part of your organization's URL (e.g., `https://dev.azure.com/yourorganizationname`) so choose something memorable. Click 'Continue'.
5. **Select a Region:** Choose the Azure region closest to your primary location or target audience. This dictates where most of your project data will be stored. Click on 'Continue'.
6. **Confirm and Create:** You'll see a summary of your choices. If everything looks good, click on "Create organization".

The Setup Process

The organization setup process might take a few minutes. Once complete, you'll be automatically taken to your Azure DevOps organization's landing page. Let's explore what you've done!

What Is an Azure DevOps Organization?

- **Central Hub:** Your Azure DevOps organization is the container for your projects and related resources.
- **User Management:** You control who has access to your organization and their specific permissions.
- **Billing:** Azure DevOps usage (beyond the included free tiers) is connected to the Azure subscription associated with your organization.

Creating Your First Project

After setting up your organization, you're ready to create your first project!

1. **Project Creation:** On the landing page, you'll see a prominent "Create project" button. Click it to initiate project creation.
2. **Project Name:** Give your project a descriptive name.
3. **Visibility:** Choose between 'Private' (accessible only to members you invite) or 'Public' (visible to the world). For most scenarios, you'll start with "Private".
4. **Version Control:** Select your preferred version control system (Git or TFVC). For this book, we will focus on Git.
5. **Work Item Process:** Choose an initial template for managing work. Opt for either 'Agile', 'Scrum', or 'Basic'. Don't stress, you can customize these later.

Click on 'Create'. Congratulations, you've brought your first Azure DevOps project into existence!

Additional Resources

- **Azure DevOps Organization Quickstart:**
  https://learn.microsoft.com/en-us/azure/devops/organizations/accounts/create-organization?view=azure-devops
- **Managing Azure DevOps Organizations:**
  https://learn.microsoft.com/en-us/azure/devops/organizations/accounts/organization-management?view=azure-devops

Next Steps

Your Azure DevOps journey has officially begun! In the next chapter, we'll delve into the fundamentals of DevOps to give you a strong conceptual foundation.

Decoding DevOps: Understanding the Fundamentals

Before we dive deep into the technical aspects of Azure DevOps, let's build a solid understanding of the core principles and philosophies that drive DevOps. This chapter is about demystifying the what, the why, and the how of this transformative approach to software development.

What is DevOps?

DevOps is more than a toolset. It signifies a cultural shift in how we think about building and delivering software. Let's break down its key aspects:

- **Collaboration:** DevOps bridges the gaps between development (Dev) and operations (Ops) teams. It promotes shared responsibility for the entire software lifecycle.
- **Automation:** DevOps stresses the use of automation to reduce manual tasks, making processes faster, more reliable, and less prone to errors.
- **Continuous Everything:** With concepts like continuous integration (CI), continuous delivery (CD), and continuous monitoring, DevOps promotes a culture of constant improvement.
- **Feedback Loops:** DevOps emphasizes the importance of rapid feedback throughout the process. This allows teams to identify problems early and adjust course swiftly.

Why DevOps Matters

Historically, software development followed a 'waterfall' model where development and operations worked in silos. This led to:

- **Slow Release Cycles:** Deployments were infrequent and often painful due to a lack of integration between the teams.
- **Finger Pointing:** Teams blamed each other for issues, creating organizational friction rather than collaboration.
- **Delayed Feedback:** Problems discovered late in the process were time-consuming and costly to fix.

DevOps aims to solve these problems, driving numerous benefits:

- **Faster Time to Market:** Accelerated release cycles help deliver features and value to users more quickly.
- **Improved Quality**: Continuous testing and integration help catch errors early, resulting in more reliable software.
- **Enhanced Collaboration:** A shared understanding of goals fosters a sense of ownership.
- **Greater Innovation:** With less time spent on firefighting, teams focus on delivering new value to customers.

Key DevOps Concepts and Practices

Let's introduce some fundamental concepts you'll keep coming across in your DevOps journey:

- **Continuous Integration (CI):** Practice of frequently merging code changes into a shared mainline to detect issues early.
- **Continuous Delivery (CD):** Extends CI, automating the process of making code changes ready for deployment to production environments.
- **Continuous Deployment:** Takes CD further, automatically deploying changes that pass tests and checks into production.
- **Infrastructure as Code (IaC):** Managing and provisioning infrastructure resources (servers, networks, etc.) through code rather than manual configuration.
- **Agile Methodologies:** Software development practices that focus on iterative development, early delivery, and continuous adaptation to change.
- **Version Control Systems (e.g., Git):** Software tools for tracking code changes, enabling collaboration and rollback to previous versions.

Changing Mindsets

DevOps isn't just about tools. A true DevOps transformation requires shifts in organizational culture:

- **Breaking Silos:** Teams need to view themselves as part of a unified process instead of isolated groups.

- **Focus on Automation:** Replace manual, repetitive tasks with automated ones whenever possible.
- **Embracing Failure as Learning:** A 'fail fast' mentality helps identify weaknesses and improve processes.

Azure DevOps as an Enabler

Azure DevOps provides a powerful platform for implementing effective DevOps practices; it brings together:

- **Azure Boards:** Agile project management tools.
- **Azure Repos:** Git-based version control.
- **Azure Pipelines:** Flexible CI/CD orchestration.
- **Azure Test Plans:** Integrated testing tools.
- **And much more!**

Additional Resources

- **The DevOps Handbook:** https://itrevolution.com/book/the-devops-handbook/
- **What is DevOps? (Microsoft Learn):** https://learn.microsoft.com/en-us/devops/what-is-devops

Next Up

Now that you have a strong grasp of the fundamentals, let's explore why DevOps has become essential in today's software landscape!

Unveiling the Power of DevOps: Why It Matters (Part 1)

In the previous chapter, we laid the groundwork for understanding DevOps. Now, it's time to explore why DevOps has become a force that drives successful software development in the modern world. In this two-part chapter, we'll uncover the transformative benefits DevOps offers and understand why organizations across industries are embracing it.

Part 1: Speed, Agility, and Innovation

Let's focus on how DevOps drives unparalleled speed, organizational responsiveness, and a culture that values innovation:

- **Faster Time to Market:** Automated processes, CI/CD pipelines, and reduced friction between teams significantly accelerate the path from coding to deployment. This empowers you to release new features and updates rapidly, keeping pace with customer needs.
- **Early Bug Detection:** As code is integrated and tested frequently, potential issues are caught at earlier stages of development. This minimizes the cost and time spent on fixing problems later in production.
- **Agility and Responsiveness:** DevOps enables teams to adapt quickly to changing requirements or market conditions. This responsiveness is critical in today's ever-evolving technology landscape.
- **Faster Feedback Loops:** Continuous feedback mechanisms, both within the team and from users, help to drive rapid iterations and improvements. This leads to a higher quality product.
- **Culture of Experimentation:** With less risk associated with changes (due to faster releases and safety nets built into the process), DevOps encourages teams to experiment. This fosters innovation and potentially ground-breaking ideas.

Real-World Examples

These benefits aren't just theoretical. Let's look at some real-life examples of companies reaping massive rewards from DevOps:

- **Amazon:** Famously implemented DevOps to achieve deployment frequencies on the order of every 11.6 seconds!
- **Netflix:** Leverages DevOps for rapid scaling and continuous delivery across its global platform, ensuring a seamless user experience.
- **Etsy:** Adopted DevOps to transform from infrequent release cycles to hundreds of deployments per day, improving their ability to deliver value to customers at a fast pace.

The Rise of Customer Expectations

DevOps' emphasis on speed and responsiveness is vital because customer expectations are ever-increasing. Users demand:

- **Rapid Innovations:** They want new features, improvements, and better experiences regularly.
- **Reliable Software:** Outages or errors are less tolerated – applications need to be robust
- **Responsiveness to Feedback:** Companies that take user feedback seriously and act on it gain a strong customer following.

The Competitive Advantage

DevOps is no longer a "nice-to-have"—it's a crucial component of business strategy. Organizations that successfully adopt DevOps practices:

- **Outpace Competitors:** Release faster and adapt quicker to market shifts.
- **Attract and Retain Talent:** Top developers want to work on modern, efficient development teams.
- **Deliver Superior Customer Value:** Drive customer loyalty and satisfaction.

Additional Resources

- **State of DevOps Reports:** https://cloud.google.com/devops

- **DORA Research Program:**
  https://cloud.google.com/devops/research

Next Up

In the next part of this chapter, we'll delve further into the benefits of DevOps, examining how it enhances reliability, scalability, and collaboration within organizations. Let's continue exploring the transformative power of DevOps!

Unveiling the Power of DevOps: Why It Matters (Part 2)

In part 1 of this chapter, we explored how DevOps drives speed, agility, and innovation. Now, let's discover how it leads to more reliable systems, improved scalability, and a culture of collaboration.

Part 2: Reliability, Scalability, and Collaboration

- **Enhanced Reliability:** DevOps' focus on continuous integration and automated testing helps catch bugs and inconsistencies early in the development process. This results in fewer production issues and a higher level of software stability.
- **Robust Scalability:** DevOps principles and practices, along with cloud-based tools, empower teams to scale their applications gracefully to handle fluctuating workloads.
- **Cross-Team Collaboration:** DevOps dismantles silos between development and operations teams, fostering a shared understanding of project goals and challenges. This increased communication often translates to a faster resolution of problems.
- **Reduced Risk:** With smaller, more frequent releases, the impact of any potential issue is minimized. If something goes wrong, the ability to roll back quickly reduces negative impacts.

Real-World Examples

- **Target:** Adopted DevOps for greater stability by reducing downtime and responding faster to incidents.
- **Microsoft:** Uses DevOps for its own Azure services, leading to increased reliability and faster feature delivery for its customers.
- **Google:** Excels at DevOps across its product suite, demonstrating the scalability of DevOps practices within a tech giant.

The Human Factor

DevOps isn't just about efficiency gains – it brings about transformative improvements within the teams themselves:

- **Improved Morale:** Reduced friction and the sense of a shared mission boost morale and job satisfaction
- **Knowledge Sharing:** Cross-functional collaboration breaks down knowledge barriers, leading to skill development across the team.
- **Ownership and Empowerment:** DevOps fosters a sense of ownership and accountability, giving team members a greater stake in the success of the product.

DevOps and the Cloud

Azure DevOps and cloud platforms form a powerful alliance. DevOps practices combined with the inherent scalability of the cloud enable:

- **On-Demand Infrastructure:** Teams can provision and de-provision resources as needed, making it easier to scale.
- **Global Reach:** Services like Azure make it possible for teams to deliver their software globally with enhanced reliability and performance.
- **Reduced Management Overhead:** Managing underlying infrastructure is simplified in cloud environments, freeing teams to focus on software development.

Additional Resources

- **Azure DevOps Case Studies:** https://azure.microsoft.com/en-us/resources/customer-stories/?products=devops
- **The Phoenix Project by Gene Kim:** A novel that illustrates the transformational power of DevOps in a relatable way. https://www.amazon.com/Phoenix-Project-DevOps-Helping-Business/dp/1942788290

It's a Journey

Realize that adopting DevOps is a process, not a single event. Success relies on continuous adaptation and optimization. Your journey starts now and this book will be your guide!

Initiating Your Project: Getting Started with Azure DevOps

With your Azure DevOps organization established and a solid understanding of DevOps principles, it's time to embark on your first Azure DevOps project! This chapter will guide you through the essential steps of setting up a new project and understanding the key elements at your disposal.

Project Initiation Steps

1. **Creating a New Project:**
   - From your Azure DevOps organization's landing page, click the prominent "Create project" button.
   - **Project Name:** Give your project a name that clearly reflects its purpose.
   - **Visibility:** Decide whether it's 'Private' (visible only to invited members) or 'Public' (open to the world). Most projects usually start as Private.
   - **Version Control:** Choose 'Git' as it's the modern standard and well-integrated with Azure DevOps.
   - **Work Item Process:** Start with a basic template like 'Agile' or 'Scrum'. You can customize these processes extensively later.
2. **Understanding Your Project Dashboard:** Once created, you'll land on your project's dashboard. Key areas include:
   - **Overview:** Summary of project activity, work items, pipelines, etc.
   - **Boards:** Central hub for work item tracking.
   - **Repos:** Where your code will reside.
   - **Pipelines:** Tool for building and deploying your code.
   - **Test Plans:** Integrated test management (if you have the appropriate access level).
   - **Wiki** (Optional): A collaborative knowledge base for your project team.

Inviting Your Team

If you're working as part of a team, here's how to invite members to your project:

1. **Project Settings:** Navigate to your Project Settings (accessed via the gear icon).
2. **Members:** Within the 'Members' section, click 'Add' and enter the email addresses of team members.
3. **Permissions:** Assign appropriate levels of access (e.g., Basic, Stakeholder).

Choosing a Template for Work Item Tracking

Azure Boards offers flexibility with work item templates:

- **Agile:** Supports iterative development, user stories, tasks, bugs, etc.
- **Scrum:** Focuses on Sprints, product backlog items, and impediments.
- **Basic:** Simplified process for those new to Azure Boards.

Recommendation: If you're new to DevOps, start with the 'Agile' or 'Basic' process. You can always tailor them as you become more familiar.

Connecting External Tools

One of the strengths of Azure DevOps is its extensibility. Connect it with popular tools your team may already rely on:

- **GitHub:** Integrate GitHub repositories for seamless code management.
- **Slack:** Get notifications and updates directly in Slack for real-time awareness.
- **Jira:** If you use Jira for issue tracking, it can be linked for a unified view.
- **Azure Marketplace:** Explore a vast array of extensions for added functionality.

Setting Up a Test Plan (Optional)

If testing is a critical component of your project, start configuring your test plans. We'll delve into Azure Test Plans in later chapters, but remember that they're readily available.

Additional Resources

- **Create a project in Azure DevOps:**
  https://learn.microsoft.com/en-us/azure/devops/organizations/projects/create-project?view=azure-devops
- **Add users to your project:**
  https://learn.microsoft.com/en-us/azure/devops/organizations/security/add-users-team-project?view=azure-devops
- **Work Item Process Templates:**
  https://learn.microsoft.com/en-us/azure/devops/boards/work-items/guidance/choose-process?view=azure-devops

Next Steps

Your project foundation is ready! Now, it's time to take a deep dive into Azure Boards, the heart of project planning and work tracking within Azure DevOps.

Section 2:
Mastering Azure Boards

Navigating Azure Boards: An Overview

Welcome to the nerve center of your Azure DevOps projects! Azure Boards is a powerful and versatile toolset that helps you visualize, plan, and track the work done by your development teams. Let's embark on an introductory tour of its core features and concepts.

Key Concepts & Terminology

Before we dive into the interface itself, let's get familiar with some fundamental Azure Boards terminology:

- **Work Items:** The building blocks of Azure Boards. A work item represents a unit of work, such as a feature, task, user story, bug, or issue.
- **Work Item Types:** Categories for your work items (e.g., 'Bug', 'Task', 'Epic'). Each type has customizable fields to capture relevant information.
- **Boards:** These provide visual interfaces for managing your work items. The main types include:
    - **Kanban Boards:** Use columns to represent different stages of your workflow (e.g., "To Do", "In Progress", "Done").
    - **Backlogs:** Prioritized lists, usually of user stories or product backlog items, vital for agile development.
    - **Sprint Boards:** Facilitate planning and monitoring tasks within a time-boxed sprint.
- **Queries:** Flexible ways to filter and list work items based on various criteria, aiding reporting and analysis.

Navigating the Azure Boards Interface

Let's dissect the typical layout when you access Azure Boards within your project:

1. **Project Navigation:** On the left, you'll find the primary navigation menu with sections for 'Boards', 'Repos', 'Pipelines', etc., allowing you to switch between different areas of Azure DevOps.
2. **Boards Hub:** The central part of the screen is your Boards hub. Here you will see:
   - **Recent and Favorite Boards:** Provides quick access to the boards you interact with most frequently.
   - **All Boards, Backlogs, Queries, Sprints:** Categorized view into different Azure Boards components.
3. **Board Content:** Each board you open occupies this section. Whether it's a Kanban board, a backlog, or a sprint view, the visual representation of your work items lives here.

Exploring a Kanban Board

Kanban boards are a popular starting point. A typical Kanban board consists of:

- **Columns:** Represent stages of your workflow (e.g., "New", "Development", "Testing", "Done").
- **Cards:** Each card represents a work item. Cards display essential information and can be dragged between columns to update their status.

Working with Backlogs

Backlogs are essential in agile methodologies:

- **Hierarchical:** Backlogs often have multiple levels (e.g., Features broken down into Epics, Epics into User Stories).
- **Prioritization:** Drag and drop items within a backlog to reflect priority.
- **Forecasting (Optional):** Some backlog views allow capacity-based planning for sprints.

Customizing Your Experience

Azure Boards is designed to be flexible:

- **Work Item Customization:** Modify fields, add new fields, or even create custom work item types if needed.
- **Column/Lane Customization (Kanban):** Rename columns, add new columns, and apply work-in-progress (WIP) limits.
- **Views:** Save customized filters or visualizations as different views within boards or backlogs.

Additional Resources

- **Azure Boards Overview - Microsoft Learn:** https://learn.microsoft.com/en-us/azure/devops/boards/get-started/what-is-azure-boards?view=azure-devops
- **Azure Boards Documentation:** https://learn.microsoft.com/en-us/azure/devops/boards/?view=azure-devops

Next Steps

Now that you have a foundational understanding of Azure Boards, let's delve deeper into the types of work items, process customization, and how boards power effective project management in the following chapter.

Deep Dive into Azure Boards: Essentials Explained

In the previous chapter, we toured the landscape of Azure Boards. Now it's time to explore the essential elements and how to use them effectively to manage your software projects.

Understanding Work Item Types

Azure Boards provides a default set of work item types (WITs) common in many agile development processes:

- **Epic:** Represents a large body of work or a high-level feature.
- **Feature:** A smaller, deliverable unit of functionality within an epic.
- **User Story:** Captures a requirement from the end-user's perspective.
- **Task:** A piece of work needed to complete a user story or feature.
- **Bug:** Represents a defect or issue in the software.
- **Issue:** A more general type for tracking problems or impediments.

Key Fields Within Work Items

Let's look at some important fields you'll find in most work items:

- **Title:** A concise summary of the work item.
- **Description:** A more detailed explanation of the problem or requirement.
- **State:** Tracks workflow progression (e.g., "New", "In Progress", "Resolved").
- **Assigned To:** The team member responsible.
- **Area Path:** Categorizes work items into functional areas of your project.
- **Iteration Path:** Associates the work item with a specific sprint or timebox.

Customizing Work Items

Azure Boards is adaptable to your specific needs. From the Process Settings for your project, you have the power to:

- **Create Custom WITs:** If you need to track things like test cases, risks, or feedback, you can create new work item types.
- **Add Fields:** Include additional data points like "Acceptance Criteria," "Due Date," or custom dropdowns by adding new fields to existing WITs.
- **Modify Workflows:** Adjust the 'State' transitions for each work item type to mirror your team's process.

Using Backlogs Effectively

Backlogs are the heart of prioritizing your work within agile methodologies. Here's how to make them work for you:

- **Nesting and Parent-Child Links:** Epics break down into Features, Features into User Stories, mirroring real-world dependencies.
- **Drag-and-Drop Prioritization:** Reorder items within the backlog to reflect the highest value work that needs to be tackled next.
- **Effort Estimation:** Add estimation fields (e.g., Story Points) to help with capacity planning.
- **Backlog Refinement:** A continuous activity where your team reviews and prepares the backlog for upcoming sprints.

Powering Sprints with Taskboards

Taskboards visualize the tasks within a sprint:

- **Swimlanes:** Use swimlanes to group work by team members, priority, or other criteria.
- **Update Tasks with Drag-and-Drop:** Easily move task cards between columns to reflect their progress.
- **Spot Bottlenecks:** Taskboards make it simple to identify if too much work is piling up in a particular workflow stage.

Queries: Unlocking Work Item Insights

Queries allow you to slice and dice work item information:

- **Creating Queries:** Use the query editor to filter work items based on fields like type, state, assignee, keywords, etc.

- **Save and Share:** Save helpful queries and share them with your team.
- **Charts and Dashboards:** Visualize query results in customizable charts and pin them to your project dashboard.

Additional Resources

- **Customize work tracking (Azure Boards):**
  https://docs.microsoft.com/en-us/azure/devops/boards/boards-work-items-customization?view=azure-devops
- **Work item queries (Azure Boards):**
  https://learn.microsoft.com/en-us/azure/devops/boards/queries/using-queries?view=azure-devops

Next Steps

With a grasp of the essentials, you're ready to create your own teams, customize work items, and leverage Azure Boards for efficient sprint execution. Let's continue our journey!

Crafting Teams and Work Items (Part 1)

In this chapter, we'll delve into how to structure your teams within Azure Boards, and then design effective work items that capture the essential details of your project's tasks.

Setting Up Teams

Azure Boards allows you to model your team structures, empowering collaboration and focused work tracking:

1. **Creating Teams:** Navigate to your 'Project Settings' and the 'Teams' section. Add a new team and give it a descriptive name.
2. **Assigning Members:** Add relevant members from your Azure DevOps organization to the team.
3. **Area Paths:** Define specific 'Area Paths' for each team. This helps categorize work items and keeps boards organized, especially in projects with multiple teams.

Configuring Team Settings

Each team has a dedicated settings page with powerful configurations:

- **Iterations:** Set up and schedule sprints or iterations as per your team's cadence.
- **Backlogs and Boards:** Configure the team's default backlog (e.g., viewing User Stories level by default), customize Kanban columns, and manage working days.
- **Capacity Planning (Optional):** Enable capacity-based planning for each team member. Use this if you track work in terms of hours or story points.

Designing Effective Work Items

Well-crafted work items are crucial for effective project tracking. Let's focus on best practices:

- **Clear and Concise Titles:** Write titles that succinctly summarize the work.

- **Meaningful Descriptions:** Provide enough detail in the description to understand the purpose, context, and acceptance criteria for the work item.
- **Utilize Rich Text:** Use formatting, links, and image attachments in descriptions for clarity.
- **Tagging and Categorization:** Use 'Area Path' and 'Iteration Path' appropriately to sort and filter. Add custom tags for additional organization.
- **Leverage Links:** Create links between related work items (e.g., a User Story to an Epic, or a Bug to a Task) for traceability.
- **Custom Fields:** If you consistently need fields like "Priority", "Severity", or "Due Date", remember you can add them to your work item types.

Work Item Templates (Optional)

To streamline work item creation, especially for recurring types, consider using templates:

- **Create Templates:** Pre-populate frequently used fields (description, tags, etc.). This saves time and promotes consistency.
- **Apply Templates:** When creating a new work item, select the relevant template to get a headstart.

Example Use Case

Let's imagine a scenario for a web development team:

- **Team:** "Frontend Developers"
- **Area Path:** "Website\Frontend"
- **Work Item Types Used:**
  - User Story (with fields like "Acceptance Criteria")
  - Bug (with fields like "Severity" and "Steps to Reproduce")
  - Task (for breaking down User Stories further)

Additional Resources

- **Configure and customize Azure Boards:**
  https://learn.microsoft.com/en-us/azure/devops/boards/sprints/assign-work-sprint?view=azure-devops
- **Work item templates in Azure Boards:**
  https://learn.microsoft.com/en-us/azure/devops/boards/backlogs/work-item-template?view=azure-devops

Next Steps

In Part 2 of this chapter, we'll dive deeper into advanced work item customization, using work items during sprint planning, and tracking progress. Stay tuned!

Crafting Teams and Work Items (Part 2)

In Part 1, we discussed setting up teams and designing well-structured work items. Now, let's see how work items power your planning processes, along with techniques to tailor them to fit your workflows and reporting needs.

Using Work Items in Sprint Planning

Here's how work items dovetail into your sprint planning process:

1. **Backlog Refinement:** Your team continuously prepares the product backlog, prioritizing, adding detail to upcoming User Stories, and breaking them down into tasks.
2. **Capacity Planning:** If using estimation fields (like Story Points), view your team's capacity for the upcoming sprint
3. **Sprint Board:** Utilize your sprint board to visualize the tasks committed to your sprint, assigning work items to team members, and updating statuses throughout.

Advanced Work Item Techniques

Let's delve into some more powerful ways to use work items:

- **Work in Progress (WIP) Limits:** Add limits to Kanban columns to visualize bottlenecks and prevent team members from getting overloaded with too many concurrent tasks.
- **State Transitions:** Customize the 'State' workflow of work items to precisely model your team's process (e.g., "In Development" -> "Ready for Testing" ->"Closed").
- **Links and Parent-Child:** Link related work items using options like:
    - **Parent/Child:** User Stories to Epics, Tasks to User Stories.
    - **Related:** Dependencies or blocks between work items.
- **Comments and @Mentions:** Use the discussion area within work items to collaborate, track decisions, and notify teammates using @mentions.

Customizing Work Items for Your Workflow

Remember, you can go further with customization! From your Project Settings:

- **Add Fields:** Create custom fields, including:
    - Text
    - Number
    - Dropdown (with predefined options)
    - Date
    - And more!
- **Modify States:** Adjust the 'State' transitions of each work item type to mirror your specific workflow.
- **Process Inheritance:** Azure Boards uses process templates (Agile, Scrum, etc.). If you make significant changes, creating a custom inherited process helps preserve your customizations against future updates.

Work Items for Reporting

Queries and Charts bring your work items to life for data-driven insights:

- **Charts on Boards/Dashboards:**
    - Burndown Charts (tracking progress towards sprint completion)
    - Pie charts to show work item distribution by type, state, etc.
- **Custom Queries:** Filter and aggregate work items for ad-hoc analysis or recurring reports.

Example: Bug Triage Process

Let's consider a custom field and state modification for a Bug work item:

- **Custom Field:** "Severity" (Dropdown: 'Critical', 'High', 'Medium', 'Low')
- **State Workflow:** "New" -> "Active" -> "Resolved" -> "Closed" (Optionally add a "Needs Verification" state).

Additional Resources

- **Use the sprint burndown in Azure Boards:**
  https://learn.microsoft.com/en-us/azure/devops/boards/sprints/sprint-burndown?view=azure-devops
- **Customize a process (Azure Boards):**
  https://learn.microsoft.com/en-us/azure/devops/organizations/settings/work/customize-process?view=azure-devops

Next Steps

With a strong grasp of teams and work items, you're ready to dive into the intricacies of sprint planning. In the next chapter, we'll discuss backlog management, forecasting, and how to kick off your sprints effectively!

Planning Your Sprint (Part 1)

Sprint planning marks a crucial cadence in agile software development. It's when the team aligns on what can be accomplished in the next iteration, translating your backlog into an actionable plan. Let's explore the key aspects of effective sprint planning using Azure Boards.

Prerequisites for Sprint Planning

Before diving into the planning session itself, ensure these are in place:

- **Agile Process:** You have a process selected (Scrum, Agile, etc.) in your project settings.
- **Defined Sprints:** Your team has set up iterations/sprints with a consistent duration (e.g., 2-week sprints).
- **Refined Backlog:** The product backlog is well-groomed, with user stories or prioritized items ready for the upcoming sprint.
- **Team Availability:** You have a good understanding of individual team members' capacities, taking into account any vacations or planned absences.

Key Steps in Sprint Planning

While practices can vary slightly, here's a common flow:

1. **Determine Sprint Goal:** Start by defining a clear, overarching goal for the sprint. What's the main value you want to deliver?
2. **Capacity Planning:** Analyze your team's available capacity for the sprint (in hours or story points). Refer to historical data (team velocity) if available.
3. **Pull Work Items from the Backlog:** Working with your team, pull the top priority items from your product backlog into your sprint backlog. This is guided by both your capacity and the sprint goal.
4. **Task Breakdown:** Break down user stories into smaller, manageable tasks. Assign these tasks to team members.
5. **Update the Sprint Board:** Visualize the sprint commitments on your sprint taskboard. Ensure columns reflect your team's workflow.

Azure Boards Tools for Planning

Azure Boards offers various features to streamline the process:

- **Backlog Views:** Use the backlog view to prioritize and drag-and-drop items directly into your sprint.
- **Forecasting (Optional):** Enable forecasting tools to visually estimate how much work you could potentially fit based on velocity.
- **Capacity Planning (Optional):** If you utilize capacity planning within your team, set the capacity for each team member.
- **Sprint Burndown Chart:** Once your sprint starts, the burndown chart helps track your progress toward the sprint goal.

Best Practices

- **Timebox the Meeting:** Set a fixed time limit (usually a few hours) to maintain focus.
- **Involve the Entire Team:** Collective participation is vital. Developers provide insights on feasibility, dependencies, and effort estimations.
- **Be Realistic:** Avoid overcommitting. Better to underpromise and overdeliver.
- **Leave Some Buffer:** Account for unplanned tasks, bugs, or potential disruptions.

Example: Let's imagine a team planning a two-week sprint.

- **Capacity:** Each team member is available for 60 hours of focused work.
- **Past Velocity:** The team usually completes 40 story points per sprint.
- **Backlog:** Top-priority items add up to approximately 45 story points.

The team might pull in the top 40 story points' worth of work and leave a few lower priority items in the backlog as a buffer.

Additional Resources

- **Plan your sprint (Azure Boards):** https://docs.microsoft.com/en-us/azure/devops/boards/sprints/sprint-planning?view=azure-devops

Next Steps

In Part 2 of this chapter, we'll delve into techniques to optimize your sprint planning, handle uncertainties, and refine your processes over time.

Planning Your Sprint (Part 2)

In Part 1, we covered the core steps of sprint planning. Let's now explore how to become more effective, address uncertainties, and how to continuously improve your sprint planning processes.

Refining Your Planning Process

- **Sprint Retrospectives:** A key part of agile; hold a retrospective at the end of each sprint. Analyze what went well, what didn't, and find areas to improve. This directly feeds back into your planning.
- **Estimate Accurately:** Use techniques like Planning Poker (if using story points) to involve the team in estimation and get more reliable forecasts.
- **Track Velocity:** Monitor your team's velocity (e.g., completed story points per sprint). This historical data will make future capacity planning more accurate.

Handling Uncertainties

- **Spikes:** Use 'Spike' work items for targeted research or prototyping to reduce uncertainty around complex tasks.
- **Flexible Scope:** While you have a sprint goal, be prepared to renegotiate the scope of the sprint if major issues or critical bugs arise.
- **Communication is Key:** Transparent communication with stakeholders helps manage expectations when uncertainties could cause delays.

Common Challenges and Solutions

Challenge	Solution
Scope Creep: Changes mid-sprint disrupt initial plans.	Define a clear change control process. Prioritize new requests for future sprints.
Dependencies: Blocked by other teams or external factors.	Identify dependencies early, maintain open communication

	channels, and have contingency plans.
Overly Optimistic Estimation: Tasks take longer than expected.	Build a buffer into your sprints, break down tasks further for more accurate estimates.
Technical Debt: Accrued work impacting velocity.	Dedicate a portion of each sprint to tackling crucial technical debt.

Beyond the Basics

Consider these enhancements if applicable to your process:

- **Risk Assessment:** During planning, identify potential risks and discuss mitigation strategies.
- **Definition of Done (DoD):** Establish a shared DoD (e.g., code reviewed, unit tests passed, etc.) to ensure work items are truly completed.
- **Team Morale:** Factor in activities that build team spirit and motivation, as this impacts productivity and sprint success.

Tools within Azure Boards

Don't forget Azure Boards has further features for refinement:

- **Tagging:** Use tags to categorize work by themes or to highlight risks.
- **Queries and Reports:** Analyze historical sprint data to identify trends and areas for improvement.

Additional Resources

- **Sprint retrospective guide (Atlassian):** https://www.atlassian.com/agile/scrum/retrospective
- **Spike in Agile Development (Scrum.org):** https://www.scrum.org/resources/blog/what-spike-agile-development

Designing Features and Epics: Thinking Big, Acting Smart

Features and epics provide the structure for breaking down large-scale initiatives within Azure Boards. Well-designed features and epics translate your product vision into manageable units of work, ensuring your sprints remain focused and deliver continuous value.

Understanding Features

- **Deliverable Value:** Features represent a unit of functionality that delivers tangible value to the end user.
- **Scope:** Larger than a User Story but should still fit within a few sprints.
- **Examples:** "Implement Search Functionality," "User Profile Creation," "Shopping Cart Checkout".

Unleashing the Power of Epics

- **Big Picture:** An epic encompasses a major objective or theme.
- **Spanning Projects or Releases:** Epics can stretch across multiple sprints, projects, or even release milestones.
- **Examples:** "Complete Website Redesign," "Mobile App Launch," "New Payment Gateway Integration"

Key Techniques for Feature and Epic Design

1. **User-Centric Focus:** Always frame features and epics in terms of the problem they solve for the user or the value they deliver.
2. **Clear Definitions:** Describe them with enough detail to provide a shared understanding across your team, but avoid getting bogged down with implementation specifics.
3. **Decomposition:** Epics break down into Features. Features, in turn, break down into User Stories. This hierarchy is key for project planning.
4. **Prioritization:** Use your product roadmap and backlog prioritization techniques to determine which epics and features are tackled first.

5. **SMART Criteria:** Consider applying SMART (Specific, Measurable, Achievable, Relevant, Time-Bound) principles to enhance your feature and epic definitions.

Leveraging Azure Boards

Azure Boards supports your process seamlessly:

- **Work Item Types:** Utilize the built-in 'Epic' and 'Feature' work item types.
- **Parent-Child Links:** Establish clear links between Epics and their Features.
- **Backlog Hierarchy:** Nest epics and features in your backlogs for easy visualization.

Best Practices

- **Size Matters:** Features should be small enough to be delivered in a reasonable timeframe, avoiding overly large epics.
- **Involve Stakeholders:** Get feedback from stakeholders and potential users on feature and epic proposals.
- **Revisit and Refine:** Epics and features may evolve. Be prepared to adjust and reprioritize as you gather new insights.
- **Tie to Initiatives:** Link top-level epics to your broader company goals or strategic initiatives.

Example Scenario

Let's imagine a project to revamp an e-commerce site. Here's a simplified breakdown:

- **Epic:** "Improve Product Discovery"
  - **Feature:** "Advanced Filtering and Sorting"
    - User Story: "Filter by price range"
    - User Story: "Sort by customer reviews"
  - **Feature:** "Enhanced Product Recommendations"
    - User Story: "Display 'You might also like' section"
    - User Story: "Suggest items based on past purchases"

Additional Resources

- **Epics, Features, and Stories (Atlassian):**
  https://www.atlassian.com/agile/project-management/epics-stories-themes
- **Writing Good Epics (Scrum.org):**
  https://www.scrum.org/resources/writing-good-epics

Next Steps

With a solid understanding of features and epics, your project backlog becomes strategically structured. Next, we'll discuss how to integrate Azure Boards with GitHub to bridge your work item tracking with your code repositories for a seamless development workflow.

Integrating Azure DevOps Boards with GitHub

When it comes to modern development, Azure Boards and GitHub are a formidable duo. This integration empowers you to bridge the gap between your project planning and your source code, bringing enhanced visibility and traceability to your workflow.

Why Connect Them?

- **Unify Workflow:** Connect GitHub commits, pull requests, and issues seamlessly to Azure Boards work items.
- **Centralized Visibility:** Get a big-picture view in Azure Boards, linking development activity directly to user stories, features, etc.
- **Traceability:** Track the full journey of code changes, from work items to pull requests through to deployment.
- **Automated Updates:** Update work item statuses automatically based on GitHub actions (e.g., close a task when a pull request is merged).

Prerequisites

- **Azure DevOps Project:** An existing project within your organization.
- **GitHub Repository:** A repository where your code will reside.
- **Permissions:** Necessary permissions in both Azure DevOps and GitHub.

Connecting Your GitHub Repository

1. **From Azure Boards:** Navigate to Project Settings -> Boards -> GitHub Connections. Click 'Connect to GitHub'.
2. **Authorization:** You'll be asked to authorize Azure DevOps to access your GitHub account and select repositories to connect.
3. **Configuration:** For each connected repository, choose:
   - **Work Item Linking Policy:** How to link Azure Boards work items with GitHub items.

     ○ **Default Work Item Types:** Work item types to automatically create in Azure Boards for commits, etc.

Linking Work Items

Here's how to associate Azure Boards work items to your GitHub activity:

- **Mentions:** Include the Azure Boards work item ID (e.g., #123) in:
  - Commit messages
  - Pull Request titles or descriptions
  - GitHub Issue titles or comments
- **Development Section (in Work Items):** Once connected, work items will have a Development section. This is where you directly create branches, initiate pull requests, or view linked commits and PRs.

Example: Let's Connect User Stories to Pull Requests

1. **In Azure Boards:** User Story #587 relates to a new search bar feature.
2. **Developer Works on a Branch:** While working on the feature, the developer names their branch something like 'feature-587-search-bar'.
3. **Creating a Pull Request:** The pull request's title or description includes a reference to "#587".
4. **Magic Happens:**
   - The pull request will be automatically reflected in the User Story's 'Development' section.
- The work item's status can be configured to update as the pull request progresses (e.g., "In Progress" when the PR is opened).

Additional Resources

- **Connect Azure Boards to GitHub (Microsoft Docs):** https://learn.microsoft.com/en-us/azure/devops/boards/github/connect-to-github
- **GitHub Marketplace - Azure Boards App:** https://github.com/marketplace/azure-boards (Provides more options)

Next Steps

With a connected workflow, you can now leverage the power of Azure Boards' views and queries to visualize and report on development progress holistically. In the next chapter, we'll explore how to get the most out of these customization features!

Optimal Board Views and Queries (Part 1)

Azure Boards offers flexibility to tailor how you visualize work. In this chapter, we'll delve into customizing board views and crafting powerful queries to extract essential information from your work items, helping you gain project insights.

Customizing Kanban Board Views

Let's start with optimizing your Kanban boards:

1. **Column Configuration:**
   - Add or remove columns to mirror your workflow stages (e.g., "Review," "In Testing")
   - Apply Work-In-Progress (WIP) limits to columns to visualize bottlenecks.
2. **Swimlanes:** Group tasks visually using swimlanes based on:
   - Teams (if you have multiple teams on a board)
   - Priority (e.g., "Urgent," "High")
   - Work item type (e.g., separate Bugs from Tasks).
3. **Card Customization:**
   - Choose which fields appear directly on your task cards to see the most relevant information at a glance.
   - Utilize styling rules to add color-coding based on criteria (e.g., blocked work items in red).

Examples

- **Development Workflow Board:** Columns reflecting "To Do," "In Development," "Code Review," "QA," "Done."
- **Support Issue Board:** Swimlanes for "Critical," "Normal," and "Low" priority issues. Cards colored red if the issue hasn't been updated in 48 hours.

Queries: Your Work Item Search Engine

Azure Boards Queries offer a structured way to find, sort, and analyze your work items.

1. **Creating Queries:** Use the 'Queries' section to create new queries.
2. **Query Editor Basics:**
   - **Field Filters:** Narrow down by fields like Work Item Type, State, Assigned To, Area Path, Iteration Path, and more.
   - **Logical Operators:** Use "AND," "OR," "Contains" to build complex filters.
3. **Save and Share:** Save helpful queries for reuse and share them across your team.

Example Queries

- **Bugs assigned to me in the current sprint:**
  - Work Item Type = Bug
  - AND Assigned To = @Me
  - AND Iteration Path = @CurrentIteration
- **Tasks overdue in the last two weeks:**
  - Work Item Type = Task
  - AND State <> Closed
  - AND Due Date < Today -14

Beyond the Basics

- **Charts from Queries:** Visualize query results in bar charts, pie charts, trend charts, and more. Pin these to your project dashboard.
- **WIQL (Work Item Query Language):** For very advanced queries, learn the syntax. This offers even greater filtering control.

Additional Resources

- **Use boards to track work in Azure Boards:**
  https://learn.microsoft.com/en-us/azure/devops/boards/boards/kanban-basics
- **Query for work items using the query editor:**
  https://learn.microsoft.com/en-us/azure/devops/boards/queries/using-queries?view=azure-devops

Optimal Board Views and Queries (Part 2)

Advanced Query Techniques

Let's explore some powerful ways to use Azure Boards queries:

- **Work Tree Results:** View work items hierarchically (e.g., see all Tasks nested under their parent User Story). Enable 'Show Parent' in your query results.
- **Filtering by Tags:** If you use tags, include them in queries (e.g., "Tags Contains 'Security'").
- **Finding Unparented Work Items:** Search for work items without links to Epics or Features to make sure everything stays connected. For example:
    - Work Item Type = Task
    - And Parent Link Does Not Contain Parent
- **Negation:** Use operators like "<>" (not equal to) and "Does Not Contain" to exclude items.

Using Queries for Reporting

- **Chart from Queries:** Once you have a useful query, convert it to a chart and pin it to your project dashboards for continuous status visibility.
- **Custom Reports (3rd-Party Extensions):** Explore extensions from the Azure DevOps marketplace for generating more advanced, tailored reports based on your work item queries.

Backlog Management with Views

Azure Boards offers specialized views within your backlog:

- **Flat List View:** Shows all items regardless of hierarchy. Useful for sorting by specific fields or bulk editing work items.
- **Mapped View:** Visualizes how work items are mapped to different Iterations (sprints). Helps with capacity planning across sprints.
- **Forecasting View:** If you are using estimation fields, the forecasting view can help you predict sprint completion.

Tips for Effective Views and Queries

- **Specificity:** Balance between too broad and too narrow results
- **Iteration:** Save different variations of your queries and views as your project needs evolve.
- **Focus:** Create views for specific purposes:
  - "Bug Triage Board"
  - "My Active Work" query
  - "Release Progress Dashboard"

Example: Release Readiness

Let's imagine you need visibility on the status of items for an upcoming release:

1. **Query: "Release Ready"**
   - Work Item Type = User Story OR Task
   - AND Iteration Path = @CurrentIteration OR Iteration Path Under @CurrentIteration
   - AND State <> Closed AND State <> Removed
2. **Kanban Board: "Release Progress"**
   - Columns: "Not Started," "In Progress," "Ready for QA," "Done"
   - Configure this board to filter based on your "Release Ready" query.

Additional Resources

- **Work item query language (WIQL) syntax:**
  https://learn.microsoft.com/en-us/azure/devops/boards/queries/wiql-syntax?view=azure-devops
- **Create reports in Azure Boards with queries:**
  https://learn.microsoft.com/en-us/azure/devops/report/powerbi/create-boards-reports-query?view=azure-devops

Next Steps

By effectively harnessing the power of boards, views, and queries, you gain invaluable insights into your project's progress. Now, it's time to move onward to the world of code repositories, starting with understanding Azure Repos, Git, and GitHub!

Section 3:
Navigating Azure Repositories

Azure Repos Demystified: A Beginner's Guide

Azure Repos is a core component of Azure DevOps, providing powerful version control capabilities for your code. Whether you're new to version control or experienced with other systems, this chapter will demystify Azure Repos and set you up for success.

Key Concepts and Terminology

- **Version Control System (VCS):** Software that tracks every change to your codebase over time, allowing you to revert to older versions, identify who made changes, and streamline collaboration.
- **Repository (Repo):** A central storage location for your project's code and related files.
- **Git:** The most popular distributed version control system, used as the foundation of Azure Repos. Understanding Git basics is vital. (We'll cover Git in detail in the next chapter).
- **TFVC:** A centralized version control system from Microsoft. Azure Repos also supports TFVC if this aligns with your team's workflow.
- **Commit:** A snapshot of your codebase at a particular point in time.
- **Branch:** A copy of your codebase, allowing you to work on changes independently from the main code line ('main' or 'master' branch).
- **Pull Request:** A mechanism to propose changes to be merged from your branch back into the main branch, fostering code review and collaboration.

Why Use Azure Repos?

- **Part of Azure DevOps:** It integrates seamlessly with other Azure DevOps services for a streamlined workflow (work items, pipelines, etc.).
- **Git or TFVC – the Choice Is Yours:** Supports both popular version control systems.
- **Cloud-Hosted:** No need to manage your own on-premises version control servers.
- **Security & Permissions:** Granular access controls to protect your code.
- **Collaboration Features:** Branching, pull requests, and built-in code review tools.

Setting Up a Repo

When you create an Azure DevOps project, you have the option to initialize it with a Git repository. If not, you can create a repo from your project's 'Repos' section.

Starting with an Empty Repo

This is the most common approach:

1. You'll get clear instructions on how to push your existing local Git codebase to Azure Repos.
2. If you're starting a brand new project, instructions for initializing your project with Git are provided.

Navigating Azure Repos

The Repos interface in Azure DevOps has several key areas:

- **Files:** Browse your code files and their history.
- **Commits:** View a list of all the commits to the repository.
- **Branches:** Manage and switch between your different development branches.
- **Pull Requests:** View and manage active pull requests for changes going into your main branch.

Additional Resources

- **Azure Repos Documentation:**
  https://learn.microsoft.com/en-us/azure/devops/repos/
- **Git tutorials:** Many resources exist, such as:
  - https://git-scm.com/docs/gittutorial
  - https://www.atlassian.com/git/tutorials

Deciphering Git and GitHub: Choosing the Right Path

In the previous chapter, we introduced Azure Repos, which can work with both Git and TFVC. Now, we take a focused look at Git, the dominant version control system in modern development, and GitHub, a popular platform built around Git.

Understanding Git

- **Distributed Power:** Unlike centralized systems, every developer has a full copy of the repository's history on their local machine. This enables offline work and faster operations.
- **Branching Made Easy:** Create branches effortlessly to experiment or work on features in isolation. Merging changes back into the main branch is streamlined.
- **Snapshots, not Diffs:** Git doesn't track differences between file versions. Instead, it takes snapshots (commits) of your entire project state.
- **Staging Area:** Provides a space to carefully select which changes to include in your next commit.
- **Command-Line Based:** While GUIs exist, the core of Git is command-line driven, offering precision and flexibility.

What about GitHub?

- **Cloud-Based Git:** GitHub is a platform for hosting Git repositories in the cloud.
- **Collaboration Hub:** Features like pull requests, issues, project wikis, and code discussions make GitHub a powerful tool for teams.
- **Open Source Powerhouse:** Hosts a vast number of public projects, fostering a vibrant open-source community.
- **Beyond Just Code:** Integrates with numerous developer tools and services.

Choosing the Right Tools

Here's a simplified guide to help you decide between different scenarios:

1. Azure Repos with Git

- **Best Fit:** Teams prioritizing tight integration with the full suite of Azure DevOps services.
- **Benefits:** Seamless connection to Azure Boards work items, Azure Pipelines, etc. Unlimited private Git repositories for free within an Azure DevOps organization.

2. GitHub

- **Best Fit:** Projects that benefit from maximum visibility and community engagement (especially open-source). Teams already heavily invested in GitHub's ecosystem.
- **Benefits:** Large developer community, rich feature set. Offers free private repositories (with limitations).

3. Hybrid: Azure Repos and GitHub

It's perfectly valid to use BOTH! For example:

- **Host the project on GitHub:** Benefit from visibility.
- **Mirror to Azure Repos:** Utilize the integrated power of Azure Boards and Azure Pipelines.

Git Essentials (Regardless of Where You Host)

To use either Azure Repos or GitHub effectively, you'll need a grasp of some key Git concepts and commands:

- **Cloning:** Getting a copy of a remote repo onto your local machine.
- **Committing:** Taking a snapshot of changes with a message.
- **Pushing:** Sending local commits to the remote repo.
- **Pulling:** Fetching updates from the remote repo to your local copy.
- **Branching & Merging:** The core workflow for working on code independently.

Additional Resources

- **Try Git interactive tutorial:** https://try.github.io
- **Pro Git Book (Free):** https://git-scm.com/book/en/v2

- **GitHub Guides:** https://guides.github.com

Next Steps

With a foundational understanding of Git, you're ready to establish your project's code environment in Azure Repos or GitHub. In the following chapter, we'll walk you through setting everything up.

Establishing Your Build Environment: Setting the Stage for Success

Before you can automate building your code with Azure Pipelines (or similar tools), you need to ensure your project can be built in a repeatable and predictable manner. This chapter focuses on setting the foundation for reliable build processes.

Key Considerations

1. **Dependencies:**
    - **External Libraries/Packages:** Does your project rely on packages from sources like NuGet, npm, or Maven? You'll need mechanisms to fetch these reliably.
    - **Other Components:** Are there internal dependencies? Do you need to build other pieces of the system first?
2. **Build Tools:**
    - **Programming Language:** Your compiler or interpreter (e.g., .NET Core SDK, Java JDK, Node.js).
    - **Build System:** Does your project use tools like MSBuild, Maven, Gradle, or custom scripts to orchestrate the build process?
3. **Build Environment:**
    - **Local Consistency:** Can everyone on the team build the project successfully on their development machines?
    - **Build Server:** Will your Azure Pipelines use Microsoft-hosted agents (clean virtual machines provided by Azure) or self-hosted agents (machines you manage)?

Local Development Environment Setup

- **Clear Documentation:** A README or similar guide in your repository should outline **all** software prerequisites and steps needed to build the project locally.
- **Automation (Ideal):** If possible, create scripts to install dependencies and streamline the build process. This minimizes manual errors and helps ensure everyone is on the same page.

Preparing Your Code

- **Build Script:** If your language/framework doesn't come with one, create a build script. This script will contain the instructions Azure Pipelines will execute.
- **Dependency Management:**
  - **Package Management Tools:** Utilize tools like NuGet (for .NET), npm (for JavaScript), or Maven (for Java) and include their configuration files in your repository.
  - **Artifact Repository:** Consider setting up your own repository for internal packages, if applicable (e.g., Azure Artifacts).

Build Environment in the Cloud

Decide between:

- **Microsoft Hosted Agents:**
  - **Pros:** Convenient, no infrastructure to maintain. Include a variety of pre-installed software.
  - **Cons:** Might need customization if you have very specific requirements.
- **Self-Hosted Agents**
  - **Pros:** Full control over configuration, ideal for specific security or compliance scenarios.
  - **Cons:** Requires maintaining your own machines or virtual machines.

Continuous Integration (CI) in Mind

As your goal is not just a working build, but an automated build process within Azure Pipelines, consider:

- **Build Triggers:** Do you want builds to start automatically on code commits? On a schedule?
- **Testing:** Include unit test execution as part of your build process for early feedback.

Example: A .NET Core Application

1. **README:** Includes instructions to install the .NET Core SDK.
2. **Build Script:** A simple MSBuild command to compile the solution.
3. **nuget.config:** Specifies package sources.
4. **CI Pipeline (Later):** Azure Pipelines will be configured to use a Microsoft-hosted agent and run your build script.

Additional Resources

- **Microsoft-hosted agents in Azure Pipelines:** https://learn.microsoft.com/en-us/azure/devops/pipelines/agents/hosted
- **Self-hosted agents in Azure Pipelines:** https://learn.microsoft.com/en-us/azure/devops/pipelines/agents/v2-windows

Next Steps

With a well-defined build environment, the next chapter will show you how to create your first repository in Azure Repos or GitHub and get your code into the cloud!

Creating Your Code Repository (Part 1)

In this chapter, we'll guide you through creating your project's code repository within your Azure DevOps organization. We'll focus on Azure Repos, but the concepts and similar steps would apply if you were using GitHub.

Prerequisites

- **Azure DevOps Project:** An existing project within your organization.
- **Local Codebase (Optional):** If you have an existing project, you'll want to get it ready to push.

Part 1: Creating the Repository and Initializing

1. **Navigate to Repos:** In your Azure DevOps project, go to the 'Repos' section.
2. **New Repository:** Click the 'New repository' button or dropdown.
   - **Repository Type:** Choose Git (most common).
   - **Name:** Give your repo a meaningful name.
   - **Initialization:** Here are your options:
     - **Empty repo:** Start from scratch
     - **Add a README:** Initialize with a basic description file.
     - **Add a .gitignore:** Choose a template appropriate for your programming language (helps exclude unnecessary files).
3. **Create!** Once you click 'Create,' your repo is ready, but it's still empty.

Initializing a Brand New Project

If you're starting completely fresh, Azure Repos provides instructions:

- **Working from the Command Line:** You'll see Git commands to create your initial files locally and push them to the remote repository.

- **Working in Your IDE:** Many IDEs (like Visual Studio Code) have Git integrations, simplifying the process of initializing your project and connecting it to Azure Repos.

Initializing with an Existing Codebase

If you have an existing project on your local machine:

1. **Locate Your Project:** Open a terminal or command prompt and navigate to your code's root directory.
2. **Initialize Git Locally:** Use the command `git init`
3. **Add the Remote:** Azure Repos provides a command like `git remote add origin <repo_url>` (replace `<repo_url>` with the actual URL of your Azure Repo).
4. **Push Your Code:** `git push -u origin main` (or 'master' if using an older naming convention). This will send your initial code to Azure Repos.

Important Considerations

- **.gitignore:** Regardless of your starting point, ensure you have a .gitignore file tailored to your project to avoid committing build artifacts, temporary files, etc.
- **Branching Strategy (Early Thinking):** While you can start with just a 'main' branch, think about how you want to use branches for features and releases in the future.

Additional Resources

- **Create a new Git repo (Azure DevOps Docs):** https://learn.microsoft.com/en-us/azure/devops/repos/git/create-new-repo
- **Git documentation:** https://git-scm.com/docs

Creating Your Code Repository (Part 2)

Adding an Existing Codebase to Your Repo

Let's assume you have a project locally, ready to be connected to Azure Repos. Recall that you'll need Git initialized in your project folder.

Step-By-Step Guide

1. **Add the Remote:**
   - Navigate to your repository in Azure Repos.
   - Click the 'Clone' button and copy the provided repository URL.
   - In your local terminal, execute: `git remote add origin <repository_url>` (replacing `<repository_url>` with the actual URL).
2. **Stage Your Changes:**
   - `git add .` (adds all changes in your project directory)
   - More controlled approach: Use `git add <specific_files>` for finer control.
3. **Commit:**
   - `git commit -m "Initial commit"` (Use a descriptive commit message)
4. **Push to Azure Repos:**
   - `git push -u origin main` (or 'master' if using older conventions). The '-u' flag sets up tracking for your local branch.

Success! Refresh your repo in Azure DevOps, and you should see your code files.

Common Scenarios & Tips

- **Large Projects:** If your initial push is very large, it might take some time.
- **Submodules:** If your project uses Git submodules, there are additional steps to initialize and update them after pushing. Refer to Git's submodule documentation.

- **Excluding Files:** Ensure your `.gitignore` file is set up to avoid unnecessary files (like build output) from cluttering your repository.

Initial Project Structure

Take this opportunity to establish the foundation of your repository's organization. Consider:

- **Top-Level Folders:** How will you structure major components of your system?
- **README.md:** A well-crafted README provides essential project information. Create this file directly in Azure Repos, or add it to your local project and push it.
- **Documentation:** If applicable, consider creating a "docs" folder for project documentation.

Branching (Early Decision)

Even if working solo, a simple branching strategy is wise. Common approaches:

- **Git Flow:** A more structured branching model (feature branches, release branches, etc.).
  https://www.atlassian.com/git/tutorials/comparing-workflows/gitflow-workflow
- **GitHub Flow:** Simpler, focused on feature branches merging back into 'main'. https://guides.github.com/introduction/flow/

Additional Resources

- **Git Basics - Adding an Existing Project to GitHub (GitHub Guides):** https://guides.github.com/introduction/git-handbook/ (Similar concepts apply to Azure Repos).

Next Steps

With your code connected to Azure Repos, you're ready to embrace the full development flow. Our next chapter delves into committing code changes strategically and effectively.

Committing Changes to Your Code (Part 1)

Commits form the backbone of your project's history in Azure Repos. Doing them effectively is essential for collaboration, debugging, and understanding how your project evolved over time.

The Workflow: Stage, Commit, Push

1. **Modify Your Code:** Make changes to your project files.
2. **Stage Changes (git add):** Selectively add files or specific changes within files to the staging area. This area is like a "pre-commit" snapshot:
   - `git add .` (Stages all modified and new files)
   - `git add <filename>` (Stages a specific file)
3. **Commit (git commit):** Create a commit with a clear and descriptive message:
   - `git commit -m "Added new search functionality"`
4. **Push (git push):** Send your committed changes from your local repository to the remote repository on Azure Repos. This is when they become visible to others (if you're collaborating).

Commit Best Practices

- **Atomic Commits:** Each commit should represent a small, logical change. This makes it easier to track and potentially revert changes if needed.
- **Clear Messages:** Your commit messages are like a logbook for the future. Explain *why* you made the change, not just *what* you changed.
- **Don't Be Afraid:** Commit often! It's easier to navigate a series of small commits than giant ones. Local commits are cheap until you push them.

Leveraging Your IDE

Most modern IDEs (like Visual Studio or VS Code) have integrated Git features:

- **Visualizing Changes:** See file modifications at a glance.
- **Selective Staging:** Stage individual lines of code easily.
- **Built-In Committing:** Commit and push directly from your IDE.

Beyond the Basics

- **git status:** Check the state of your working directory and what's staged.
- **git diff:** See the differences between your working files and the last commit.
- **Amend Previous Commit:** Use `git commit --amend` to modify your most recent commit instead of creating a brand new one (use with care).

Example Scenario

Let's say you're tasked with adding a basic sorting feature to a product listing:

1. **Small Steps:** You might break this down into commits like:
   - "Implement sort function on product data"
   - "Add dropdown UI element to select sort type"
   - "Wire up sorting logic to UI"
2. **Testing Locally:** Commits don't have to be "finished" code, but test locally to ensure you aren't breaking anything before pushing.

Additional Resources

- **Try Git online interactive tutorial:** https://try.github.io/
- **Git documentation (git commit):** https://git-scm.com/docs/git-commit

Next Steps

Understanding the commit workflow is one side of the coin. In Part 2, we'll look at how to undo changes when needed, both locally and remotely, if things don't go quite as planned.

Committing Changes to Your Code (Part 2)

Undoing Changes Locally (Before Pushing)

- **Modify the Last Commit:**
  - `git commit --amend` to change files or your commit message. Use this for simple tweaks immediately after committing.
- **Unstage Changes:**
  - `git reset <file>` to unstage a file from the staging area. Changes remain in your working directory.
- **Discard Changes (Caution):**
  - `git checkout -- <file>` discards modifications to a file. This action is often harder to reverse!

Undoing Changes Remotely (After Pushing)

- **Reverting a Commit:**
  - `git revert <commit-hash>` creates a new commit that undoes the changes of a previous commit. This preserves history rather than erasing the past.
- **Force Pushing (Use with Extreme Care):**
  - `git push -f origin <branch>` overwrites remote history. Can cause issues for collaborators. Only use this in specific scenarios if you really know what you're doing.

Stashing: When You Need a Quick Pause

- `git stash` temporarily saves your current uncommitted changes so you can switch contexts or branches cleanly.
- `git stash pop` re-applies your most recently stashed changes.

Example: Oops! I Committed Too Early

1. **Don't Panic:** Most things are fixable in Git.
2. **Identify What Needs Fixing:**
   - Did you miss files in the commit? Use `git add` and `git commit --amend`.

- Did you make a coding error you need to undo? Modify the files and create a new commit.
- Did you commit to the wrong branch? Well, that's where branching strategies come in (more on this later).

Branching as Your Safety Net: (Preview)

Branching allows you to experiment in isolation. You can always switch back to your 'main' branch before pushing, ensuring your "official" history stays clean. We'll cover branching soon!

Additional Resources

- **Undoing Things in Git (Atlassian Tutorial):** https://www.atlassian.com/git/tutorials/undoing-changes
- **Git Stash: The Basics** https://git-scm.com/book/en/v2/Git-Tools-Stashing-and-Cleaning

Initiating a Pull Request: Fostering Seamless Collaboration

Pull requests (PRs) lie at the heart of how teams review, discuss, and integrate code changes in a controlled manner. While platforms like Azure Repos or GitHub provide the mechanism, it's the team process surrounding them that makes them powerful.

The Essence of a Pull Request

1. **Your Work on a Branch:** Instead of committing directly to 'main,' you develop on a feature branch.
2. **Propose Merging:** The pull request signals your intent to merge your branch into the target branch (usually 'main').
3. **Discussion and Review:**
   - Teammates see your changes in context and leave comments.
   - You can address feedback with further commits on your branch.
4. **Approval:** Required reviewers sign off.
5. **Merge:** Your changes seamlessly become part of the main codebase.

Why Pull Requests?

- **Code Quality:** Enforce code reviews before integration.
- **Knowledge Sharing:** Teammates learn from each other's code.
- **Maintainability:** A history of discussions around a change is invaluable.
- **Safety Net:** You can experiment with more confidence when your feature branch is isolated.

Initiating a Pull Request in Azure Repos

1. **Branch & Push:** Once you've committed to your branch and pushed it to Azure Repos, the option to create a PR will appear.
2. **Description:** Provide a title and detailed description of the changes, including:

○ What problem does this solve?
○ How did you implement it?
○ Any testing instructions

3. **Reviewers:** Assign team members who should review your changes.
4. **Work Items :** Link to Azure Boards work items associated with these changes (great for traceability).

Best Practices for Smooth Pull Requests

- **Small & Focused:** Each PR should address a single issue or feature.
- **Complete Thoughts:** Even if not 100% done, a PR should represent a logical chunk of work ready for review.
- **Draft PRs:** Create a "Draft" pull request to signal work-in-progress and get early feedback.
- **Self-Review:** Review your own changes before assigning reviewers.

Additional Resources

- **Azure Repos - Review code with pull requests:**
  https://docs.microsoft.com/en-us/azure/devops/repos/git/pull-requests-overview?view=azure-devops
- **GitHub - About pull requests:**
  https://docs.github.com/en/pull-requests/collaborating-with-pull-requests/proposing-changes-to-your-work-with-pull-requests/about-pull-requests

Next Steps

Pull requests unlock the power of teamwork. Next, we'll discuss how to effectively work on your code locally in conjunction with the remote repository.

Local Code Workflows (Part 1)

While Azure Repos provides the central repository, much of your coding happens on your local machine. A fluid workflow is key to an efficient development process.

Key Components

1. **IDE or Text Editor:** Your chosen code development environment (e.g., Visual Studio, Visual Studio Code, etc.).
2. **Git Client:**
   - **Command Line:** Many devs prefer direct interaction with Git commands.
   - **GUI Tools:** Built into your IDE or standalone (like SourceTree, GitKraken). These offer visual aids.
3. **Your Project's Code (Local Copy):** This is your working directory.

The Basic Workflow

The following assumes you already have an Azure Repo set up.

1. **Cloning:**
   - `git clone <your_repo_url>` This fetches the entire repo to your local machine for the first time.
2. **Branching (Day One):** Create a branch for your first feature or task
   - `git checkout -b <branch_name>` (creates and switches to the branch).
3. **Develop & Commit:**
   - Make changes, stage them, and commit regularly. You're working locally.
4. **Pushing:**
   - `git push -u origin <branch_name>` (First push sets up tracking).
   - Subsequent pushes to the same branch only need `git push`.
5. **Pull Request:** When you're ready, initiate a pull request from Azure Repos to start the code review process.

Example: Adding a New Page to a Website

1. **Branch:** `git checkout -b add-about-page`
2. **Code:** Edit HTML, CSS, JavaScript locally. Test in your browser.
3. **Commit Often:** `git add . git commit -m "Basic about page layout"`
4. **Push:** `git push -u origin add-about-page`
5. **Pull Request:** Create a PR in Azure Repos, linking to any relevant work items.

Additional Considerations

- **Staying Up-to-Date:** Before starting work, consider fetching updates to your 'main' branch and merging them into your feature branch to avoid conflicts later. We'll cover this soon!
- **IDE Integration:** Most IDEs offer seamless Git functionality.
- **Remote Changes:** Before pushing, a `git pull` is a good habit to ensure you're not accidentally overwriting someone else's changes.

Additional Resources

- **Git documentation (Basic Workflow):** https://git-scm.com/docs/everyday
- **Visual Studio Code - Git Integration:** https://code.visualstudio.com/docs/editor/versioncontrol

Next Steps

A solid grasp of local basics sets the foundation. In Part 2, we'll explore the crucial skill of keeping your development branch in sync with the ever-evolving codebase.

Local Code Workflows (Part 2)

Scenario: The Evolving Codebase

While you're working on your feature branch, it's likely others on your team are making changes and merging them into 'main' (or your target branch). You need to integrate those changes to avoid nasty conflicts during your pull request.

Key Git Commands for Staying Updated

1. **Fetch:**
   - `git fetch` Downloads updates from the remote repo *without* merging them into your local branch. Keeps you aware of what's out there.
2. **Pull:**
   - `git pull` Fetches updates *and* attempts to merge them into your current working branch.
3. **Merge:**
   - If `git pull` results in a merge conflict (changes clashing), you'll need to manually resolve them and create a merge commit.

A Workflow for Keeping Your Branch Up-to-Date

1. **Before You Start Coding (Best Practice):**
   - `git checkout main` (Switch to your main branch)
   - `git pull` (Grab the latest from the remote)
   - `git checkout <your-feature-branch>` (Switch back to your feature branch)
   - `git merge main` (Bring in updates to your branch)
2. **Periodically while working:**
   - Repeat the above process to incorporate changes as they happen on 'main.' Fixes merge conflicts early!

Resolving Merge Conflicts

- **Your IDE to the Rescue:** Most IDEs have tools to compare changes, choose which version to keep, and finalize the merge.
- **Learn the Basics:** Understanding manual merge conflict resolution in your text editor is a valuable skill for those trickier cases.

Example: Two People Edit the Same Page

1. You both start with the same initial 'main' code.
2. You edit the contact info on your branch.
3. Your teammate updates the product description (and their changes get merged into 'main').
4. When you pull/merge 'main' into your branch, Git might detect a conflict in that file.
5. You resolve this, deciding whose contact info change is correct (or how to combine changes).

Rebase: An Alternative (Advanced)

Rebasing rewrites history, making your commits sit on top of the latest 'main'. It often creates a cleaner commit graph, but use it with caution if you've already pushed your branch (others will need to adjust).

Additional Resources

- **Git Merge vs. Rebase:** https://www.atlassian.com/git/tutorials/merging-vs-rebasing
- **Git documentation (Merge):** https://git-scm.com/docs/git-merge

Next Steps

A smoothly integrated branch makes pull requests less stressful. In our next installment, we'll explore scenarios when you might need to work with multiple remote repositories simultaneously.

Local Code Workflows (Part 3)

Scenario: Working with Multiple Remotes

Sometimes a project might necessitate pulling code from (or contributing to) repositories beyond your primary Azure Repo. For instance:

- **Dependencies:** Your project uses external libraries hosted on a separate repo.
- **Forked Projects:** You're maintaining a fork of an open-source project on GitHub and proposing changes back upstream.

Git Remotes

- **Remote:** A short name representing the URL of a remote repository.
- **origin:** The default remote name, usually pointing to your main Azure Repo.
- **Adding Remotes:** `git remote add <name> <url>`

Example: Using an External Library

1. **Add the Remote:**
   - `git remote add awesome-library https://github.com/some-org/awesome-library.git`
2. **Fetch Updates from the Library:**
   - `git fetch awesome-library`
3. **Merge a Specific Branch:**
   - `git merge awesome-library/stable` (This brings changes into your local branch)

Contributing Upstream (if applicable)

- **Forking on GitHub/Azure DevOps:** Creates a copy of the repo under your account.
- **Add Your Fork as a Remote:** For pushing your changes to your fork.

- **Standard Pull Request Flow:** Create branches, push, and submit pull requests to the upstream repo.

Workflow Complexity

Remember, each additional remote adds a layer of complexity when syncing your code. Strive to keep things simple when possible.

Working with Submodules

Submodules allow you to embed other Git repositories within your project. They're best for true, read-only dependencies.

- **Adding a submodule:** `git submodule add <url> <path-within-your-repo>`
- **Updating submodules:** `git submodule update —init —recursive`

Be aware: Submodules require specific commands to initialize and update them.

Additional Resources

- **Git Remotes:** https://git-scm.com/docs/git-remote
- **Git Submodules:** https://git-scm.com/docs/git-submodule

Next Steps

With these tools, you can navigate more complex project relationships. Next, we'll turn to the powerful capability of understanding the history of your codebase within Azure Repos.

Unraveling Commit History (Part 1)

Commit history is your project's change log. Learning to read it effectively is an essential skill when working with Azure Repos.

Where to Find History

- **Azure Repos:** Provides a web interface to browse your repo's history, view changes within commits, and more.
- **Your IDE:** Most IDEs integrate Git history visualization tools.
- **Command Line Power (git log):** The `git log` command offers granular control for inspecting commits on your local machine.

Key Concepts

- **Each Commit is a Snapshot:** Includes not just modified lines but the entire project state, author, date, and a commit message.
- **Commit Hash:** A unique identifier for each commit (e.g., '8s8d7f98s7df9').
- **Branches Are Pointers:** Your 'main' branch is merely a pointer to the most recent commit on the primary development line.

Basic Exploration

Let's start with some practical ways to examine your history

1. **Azure Repos Interface:**
   - Navigate to your repo in Azure DevOps.
   - Click 'Commits' in the left-hand menu. You'll see a list of recent commits.
   - Click a commit to see changed files and the 'diff' (what changed).
2. **git log (Command line):**
   - `git log`: Shows commits in reverse chronological order.
   - `git log --oneline`: Condensed view, great for skimming.
   - `git log --graph`: Starts to visualize branching structure

Example: Who Changed That Code?

1. **Find the Culprit Line:** Locate the troublesome code.
2. **Blame!:** Azure Repos has a 'Blame' view (similar feature in many IDEs) to show each line's last commit and author.

Additional Resources

- **Git log (Git documentation):** https://git-scm.com/docs/git-log
- **Azure Repos - View git history:**
  https://docs.microsoft.com/en-us/azure/devops/repos/git/view-git-history?view=azure-devops

Next Steps

Knowing which commit introduced a bug is one thing, but sometimes you need to dig deeper into *how* that change happened. In Part 2, we'll learn to compare differences and potentially travel back in time!

Unraveling Commit History (Part 2)

Diffing: The Key to Understanding Changes

- **Azure Repos Interface:** The 'diff' view within a commit shows line-by-line changes between a file's older and newer versions.
- **git diff (Command Line):** Offers flexible ways to compare:
  - `git diff <commit1> <commit2>`: Changes between two specific commits
  - `git diff <branch> <other-branch>`: Net changes between branches.
  - `git diff -- <file>`: Changes of a file between your working copy and the last commit.

Scenario: A Feature Disappears

1. **Isolate:** Try to determine roughly when the feature worked correctly (a range of commits).
2. **Binary Search with History:** Use `git diff` or Azure Repos to compare a known-good and a broken commit, helping narrow down the culprit commit.

Reverting Changes (Tread Carefully!)

- **Temporary Checkout (Non-Destructive):**
  - `git checkout <commit-hash>` lets you inspect a past project state.
  - Get back to your branch with `git checkout <branch-name>`.
- **Creating a Revert Commit (New Commit):**
  - `git revert <commit-hash>` This introduces a new commit that effectively undoes the changes of the old commit. History is preserved.

When Not To Rewrite Published History

If you've *already pushed* commits to a shared branch, rewriting them can cause havoc for your team. Reverting is usually the safer option in collaborative scenarios.

Visual Tools Make Life Easier

- **Git History in your IDE:** Most IDEs offer rich graphical visualizations of your project's history.
- **Standalone Tools:** Software like GitKraken or SourceTree provide intuitive interfaces focused on version history.

Example Workflow: Undoing a Recent Mess

1. **Whoops!:** You realize recent commits broke something important.
2. **Identify the Good:** Find the last commit hash where things definitely worked.
3. **Revert in Azure Repos:** Often the web interface has a "Revert" button for creating a new commit to undo the problematic one.

Additional Resources:

- **Git diff Documentation:** https://git-scm.com/docs/git-diff
- **Git checkout Documentation:** https://git-scm.com/docs/git-checkout

Next Steps

Understanding the log is one part of the equation. Sometimes, keeping that log tidy and organized is key, which we'll cover in our next chapter on repository maintenance.

Repository Maintenance: Keeping Your Workspace Tidy and Efficient

Why Maintenance Matters

Like a neglected house, a messy repository incurs 'technical debt':

- **Hard to Navigate:** Finding things gets difficult as unnecessary files and abandoned branches accumulate.
- **Knowledge Loss:** Without clear conventions, the "why" behind the codebase erodes.
- **Risk of Conflicts and Errors:** Confusion and outdated elements can break builds or create unexpected behavior.

Key Areas to Address

1. **Branch Hygiene:**
   - **Delete Old Branches:** Merged branches clutter your view. Regularly cleanup.
   - **Naming Conventions:** `feature/new-login-ui`, `bugfix/cart-checkout-issue` are much clearer than random branch names.
2. **File Organization:**
   - **Clear Folder Structure:** Is it easy to guess where different components of your system live?
   - **Delete Useless Stuff:** Leftover test code, unused assets, etc.
   - **README File:** A good README at the root of your repo is developer gold.
3. **Tagging:**
   - **Mark Releases:** Use tags (e.g., 'v1.0.2') to create snapshots of your codebase at important milestones.
4. **Commit Hygiene:**
   - **Atomic Commits:** Remind yourself and your team! Each commit should be a focused unit of change.
   - **Meaningful Messages:** Future developers (and your future self) will thank you!

Advanced Pruning Techniques (Use with Care)

- **Squashing Commits:** Rewrites history to combine multiple commits into one. Makes a linear history but can be disruptive for collaboration.
- **Git Filter-Repo:** Tool to purge large files, sensitive information, etc., permanently from your history.

Automation Helps

- **Linter Tools:** Can enforce file organization or code formatting, helping with consistency.
- **Pre-Commit Hooks:** Scripts that run before a commit, potentially catching errors or policy violations.

It's a Cultural Thing

Establishing good maintenance habits within your team is as essential as the tools themselves.

Additional Resources

- **Git Tagging:** https://git-scm.com/docs/git-tag
- **Git Filter-Repo:** https://github.com/newren/git-filter-repo

Next Steps

With a tidy version control foundation, we're ready to take the next significant step: automating the building of your software with Azure Pipelines!

Section 4:
Orchestrating Code Builds and Deployments with Azure Pipelines

Mastering DevOps Pipelines: A Comprehensive Overview

What is a DevOps Pipeline?

In essence, a pipeline is a series of defined steps that transform your code into a deployable product and release it to target environments. Consider it an assembly line for your software delivery.

Key Components

1. **Source Control:** Azure Pipelines integrates tightly with Azure Repos, but it can also work with repositories like GitHub.
2. **Triggers:** What kicks off a pipeline? Common triggers include:
   - **Code Push:** A new commit to a specific branch.
   - **Scheduled:** Run on a schedule (e.g., nightly builds).
   - **Manual:** A developer or release manager starts it.
3. **Stages:** Pipelines are often grouped into stages representing logical divisions (e.g., "Build," "Test," "Deploy to Production")
4. **Jobs:** A job is a collection of tasks that execute together on an agent or server.
5. **Tasks:** The atomic building blocks within a job. Tasks perform actions like:
   - Compiling Code
   - Running Tests
   - Packaging Artifacts
   - Deploying to an Environment
   - Triggering External Processes

6. **Artifacts:** Files or packages produced by a pipeline, passed between stages (e.g., your compiled web app, test results).

Core Benefits

- **Automation & Reproducibility:** Eliminates error-prone, manual steps. Once a pipeline is working, it performs tasks the same way, every time.
- **Early Feedback:** Integrate testing into your pipeline to catch problems quickly.
- **Faster Release Cadence:** Automation speeds up deployment, allowing for more frequent, smaller updates.
- **Audit Trail:** Pipelines keep track of what was deployed, when, and by whom.

Types of Pipelines in Azure DevOps

- **Build Pipelines (CI):** Focus on taking your code, compiling, testing, and producing a releasable artifact. This is the heart of Continuous Integration (CI).
- **Release Pipelines (CD):** Focus on deploying the artifacts produced by build pipelines into different environments (dev, staging, production), often with approval gates and additional steps. This is your Continuous Deployment/Delivery (CD) mechanism.

Streamlining Release Management with Azure DevOps

Builds vs. Releases (Recap)

- **Build Pipelines (CI):** Take your code and produce deployable artifacts.
- **Release Pipelines (CD):** Manage the process of getting those artifacts into various environments (testing, staging, production), often with approvals and complex logic.

Why Dedicated Release Management Matters

- **Environment-Specific Configurations:** Settings often change between environments (database connection strings, feature flags, etc.). Release pipelines manage this.
- **Approval Gates:** Insert manual approval points before deploying to sensitive environments, ensuring review by stakeholders.
- **Orchestration Beyond Code:** Release pipelines can execute scripts, update databases, trigger notifications, and more.
- **Auditability:** Clear history of what was deployed, when, and by whom.

Key Concepts in Azure Release Pipelines

- **Stages:** Logical groupings of deployment steps ("Deploy to Dev," "Deploy to Staging," etc.).
- **Approvals:** Pause the pipeline's execution until a designated user or group gives the green light. Can be pre- or post-deployment.
- **Gates:** Automated checks based on various conditions (e.g., query external systems, wait for test results).
- **Deployment Strategies:** Blue-green, canary, rolling - different strategies supported.

Example: A Typical Release Flow

1. **Build Pipeline Triggers Release:** A successful build completion kicks off the release pipeline.
2. **Stage: Dev Deployment:**

- Artifact from build is deployed to a development environment.
- Automated tests might run (integration tests).

3. **Stage: Approval for Staging:**
   - Release pauses for designated stakeholders to review.

4. **Stage: Staging Deployment:**
   - If approved, deployment proceeds to the staging environment. More robust testing may happen here.

5. **Stage: Production Deployment**
   - Final approval needed.
   - Production deployment executes with a chosen strategy (e.g., blue-green to minimize downtime).

Additional Resources

- **Azure DevOps Release Pipelines Documentation:** https://docs.microsoft.com/en-us/azure/devops/pipelines/release/?view=azure-devops
- **Blue-Green Deployment Strategies:** https://martinfowler.com/bliki/BlueGreenDeployment.html

Understanding the Essence: Builds vs. Releases

Focus and Outcomes

Feature	Build (CI)	Release (CD)
Focus	Code Transformation	Deployment to Environments
Input	Source Code	Build Artifacts
Output	Artifacts (compiled code, packages, etc.)	Deployed Application
Triggers	Often code changes, schedule-based	Build completion, manual, external events
Scope	Single code change, feature branch	Orchestration across environments, may bundle changes

An Analogy: Baking a Cake

- **Build:** Represents the act of mixing ingredients, baking, and producing the finished cake. These are the steps to transform your code into something deployable.
- **Release:** Is about packaging the cake, transporting it to a party, cutting it, and serving it to guests. This involves getting your application into various environments.

Key Points

- **Not Mutually Exclusive:** Well-defined DevOps workflows leverage both. Builds supply the ingredients; releases get them to the right customers.
- **Artifacts are the Bridge:** The output of your build pipeline (*the cake*) becomes the input for your release pipeline.

- **Frequency:** Build often! Typically, you'll have many builds for each release as you develop and test features.
- **Control Flow:** Releases often incorporate approvals and gates for control, especially in higher-level environments (staging, production).

Conceptual Example

Build Pipeline

1. Triggered by code push to the 'main' branch.
2. Pulls the latest code.
3. Compiles your application.
4. Executes unit tests.
5. Packages the result into an artifact.

Release Pipeline

1. Triggered by a successful build.
2. **Stage: Development**
   - Deploys the artifact to the dev environment
   - Runs smoke tests (basic functionality check)
3. **Stage: Staging**
   - Approval gate: QA team signs off.
   - Deploys to staging for more thorough testing.
4. **Stage: Production**
   - Approval gate: Release manager authorizes
   - Deploys using a production-safe strategy

Additional Resources

- **Thoughtworks - Continuous Integration vs. Continuous Delivery vs. Continuous Deployment:** https://www.thoughtworks.com/continuous-integration-delivery-deployment

Next Steps: With the distinction between builds and releases clear, it's time to start crafting a simple build pipeline. We'll focus on compiling your code, running tests, and producing that essential artifact for later deployment!

Crafting Your Build Pipeline (Part 1)

Prerequisites

- An Azure DevOps project with a code repository.
- A basic understanding of build steps for your chosen programming language.
- A willingness to experiment!

Step 1: Creating the Pipeline

1. **Navigate to Pipelines:** In your Azure DevOps project, go to the 'Pipelines' section.
2. **Click 'New Pipeline':** This starts the pipeline creation wizard.
3. **Choose Source:** Select where your code is located (Azure Repos Git, GitHub, etc.). Follow the prompts to connect to your repository.
4. **Configure:** Azure DevOps will often try to guess the correct build template based on your code. You can choose a predefined template (like .NET, Node.js) or start with an 'Empty job.'

Step 2: Hello, World Pipeline

Let's assume your repository has a simple project. If Azure DevOps doesn't provide a perfect starting point, your initial pipeline might look roughly like this (we'll be using YAML syntax):

```
trigger:

- main  # Trigger on commits to the main branch


pool:

 vmImage: 'ubuntu-latest'  # Your build agent's OS


steps:

- script: echo Hello, Azure Pipelines! # A basic
display command
```

Step 3: Understanding the Structure

- **trigger:** Defines when your pipeline runs. For now, we build on code changes to the 'main' branch.
- **pool:** Specifies the type of build agent your pipeline needs (Windows, Linux, macOS). Here, we're using a Linux Ubuntu machine.
- **steps:** The heart of your build. Each step is a task executed by the build agent.

Step 4: Executing the Build

- **Save the Pipeline:** Give your pipeline a name and click 'Save and run'.
- **Behold the Power:** Azure DevOps should now spin up a build agent and execute your simple step. You'll see real-time logs!

Step 5: Replacing Placeholders

Now, let's substitute the 'echo' with the actual build commands for your project type. Example scenarios:

- **.NET Project:**

```
- task: DotNetCoreCLI@2

  inputs:

    command: 'build'
```

- **Node.JS Project:**

```
- task: NodeTool@0

  inputs:
```

```
        versionSpec: '16.x'  # Example

- script: npm install

- script: npm run build
```

Additional Resources

- **Azure Pipelines Task Library:**
  https://docs.microsoft.com/en-us/azure/devops/pipelines/tasks/
- **YAML Schema for Pipelines:**
  https://docs.microsoft.com/en-us/azure/devops/pipelines/yaml-schema

Next Steps

A simple build is the first milestone! In Part 2, we'll enhance our pipeline by adding test execution and the generation of those all-important build artifacts.

Crafting Your Build Pipeline (Part 2)

Step 1: Integrate Unit Tests

Assuming your project has unit tests, let's get them running during the build:

- **Find Your Test Task:** Azure Pipelines has built-in tasks for many testing frameworks:
    - .NET: DotNetCoreCLI@2 (with command: 'test')
    - Node.js: npm (with npm run test)
    - Python: python -m unittest (adjust accordingly)
- **Fail the Build (if needed):** Most test tasks allow you to configure the pipeline to fail if tests don't pass. This enforces quality early!

Example: .NET Core Project

```
steps:
# ... previous build steps ...

- task: DotNetCoreCLI@2
  displayName: 'Execute Unit Tests'
  inputs:
    command: test
    projects: '**/*Tests/*.csproj' # Adjust if your
tests are in a different location
    arguments: '--configuration
$(BuildConfiguration)'
```

Step 2: Publishing Test Results

- **Dedicated Task:** Use the PublishTestResults@2 task. This makes test results and analysis viewable within Azure DevOps.

```
steps:
# ... previous steps ...

- task: PublishTestResults@2
```

```
    displayName: 'Publish Test Results'
    inputs:
      testResultsFormat: 'JUnit' # Or NUnit, VSTest
etc.
      testResultsFiles: '**/TEST-*.xml'  # Pattern for
finding result files
```

Step 3: Building the Artifact

The goal of your build pipeline is to produce the deployable package. How you do this depends on your technology:

- **Web Apps: Tasks for zipping folders, containerizing (Docker), etc.**
- **Libraries: Package management tools (NuGet, npm…)**

Example: Packaging a Python Application

```
steps:
# ... previous steps ...

- task: ArchiveFiles@2
  displayName: 'Archive application'
  inputs:
    rootFolderOrFile: $(Build.SourcesDirectory) #
Where your web app code lives.
    includeRootFolder: false
    archiveFile:
$(Build.ArtifactStagingDirectory)/$(Build.BuildId).z
ip
```

Step 4: Publishing the Artifact

- **The PublishBuildArtifacts@1 task:** This task uploads your generated artifact, making it accessible to release pipelines or for manual download.

```
- task: PublishBuildArtifacts@1
```

```
displayName: 'Publish Artifact'
inputs:
  pathtoPublish:
'$(Build.ArtifactStagingDirectory)'
  artifactName: 'drop'
```

Additional Resources

- **Azure Pipelines - Unit Testing:**
  https://docs.microsoft.com/en-us/azure/devops/pipelines/test/unit-testing-overview
- **Azure Pipelines - Artifacts:**
  https://docs.microsoft.com/en-us/azure/devops/pipelines/artifacts

Implementing GitHub Pipelines (Part 1)

What are GitHub Actions?

- GitHub Actions is a workflow automation system built directly into GitHub.
- Like Azure Pipelines, it focuses on automating CI/CD processes triggered by events within your repository.
- Workflows are defined using .YAML files, similar to Azure Pipelines.

Why Consider GitHub Actions?

- **Tight Integration:** If your code already lives on GitHub, Actions provides a close-knit experience.
- **Marketplace:** GitHub has a rich marketplace of reusable actions, streamlining common tasks.
- **Open Source Friendly:** Many open-source projects heavily utilize Actions for their workflows.

Key Concepts (Analogous to Azure Pipelines)

- **Workflows:** Defined in .YAML files living within your repository.
- **Jobs:** A collection of steps within a workflow.
- **Steps:** Individual tasks using pre-built actions or custom scripts.
- **Runners:** The machines (GitHub-hosted or self-hosted) that execute your workflows.

Basic Workflow Structure

Workflows are stored within the `.github/workflows` directory in your repository:

```
name: My Build Pipeline  # Name of your workflow

on:
  push:
    branches: [ main ]  # Trigger on commits to the
main branch
```

```
jobs:
  build-job:  # Name of a job
    runs-on: ubuntu-latest

    steps:
    - uses: actions/checkout@v3   # Check out your
code
      # More steps here: build, test, etc.
```

Example: Building a Node.js Project

```
name: Node.js CI

on: [push]

jobs:
  build:
    runs-on: ubuntu-latest

    steps:
      - uses: actions/checkout@v3
      - uses: actions/setup-node@v3
        with:
          node-version: '16'
      - run: npm install
      - run: npm run build
      - run: npm test
```

Additional Resources

- **GitHub Actions Documentation:**
  https://docs.github.com/en/actions
- **GitHub Actions Marketplace:**
  https://github.com/marketplace?type=actions

Implementing GitHub Pipelines (Part 2)

Deployment with GitHub Actions

The beauty of GitHub Actions lies in the marketplace of prebuilt actions. Here's a simplified example of deploying a Node.js web app to an Azure Web App:

```
jobs:
  # ... Your build job ...

  deploy:
    needs: build  # Ensure the build job runs first
    runs-on: ubuntu-latest

    steps:
      - uses: actions/checkout@v3
      - uses: azure/webapps-deploy@v2
        with:
          app-name: 'my-web-app'        # Name of
your Azure Web App
          publish-profile: ${{
secrets.AZURE_WEBAPP_PUBLISH_PROFILE }}
```

Important Notes:

- **Needs:** For job ordering (`deploy` waits for `build` to complete successfully).
- **Secrets:** Sensitive data (like your Azure deployment credentials) are stored securely within GitHub's project settings.

Deployment Scenarios

GitHub Actions are versatile. Consider these options:

- **Azure Deployments:** Rich set of actions for deploying to Azure resources (Web Apps, VMs, Functions, etc.)

- **Container Registries:** Actions for pushing Docker images to registries like Azure Container Registry or Docker Hub.
- **Infrastructure as Code (IaC):** Actions to interact with Terraform, ARM templates, etc.
- **Third-Party Platforms:** Actions for deploying to Heroku, AWS, and more.

Choosing between Azure Pipelines and GitHub Actions

Here's a simplified decision guide:

Lean towards Azure Pipelines if:

- You're heavily invested in the Azure DevOps ecosystem.
- You need more granular control or features unique to Azure Pipelines release pipelines.
- You're deploying complex multi-component applications across many Azure resources.

Lean towards GitHub Actions if:

- Your code is on GitHub and you want a streamlined experience within that environment.
- Your CI/CD process is relatively self-contained within your repository.
- You leverage many open-source libraries that provide GitHub Actions.

It's Not Always Either/Or!

You can use Azure Pipelines for building and GitHub Actions for deployment. Or, trigger an Azure release pipeline from a GitHub Action – these tools can be orchestrated to your advantage!

Additional Resources

- **Azure Actions for GitHub Workflows:** https://docs.microsoft.com/en-us/azure/developer/github/github-actions
- **GitHub Actions Marketplace (Filter by Deployment):** https://github.com/marketplace?type=actions&query=deployment

Next Steps

With the ability to build and deploy, you have a solid CI/CD foundation on GitHub! Next, we'll dive into crafting release pipelines in Azure DevOps, where we'll focus on multi-environment orchestration and approvals.

Constructing a DevOps Release Pipeline (Part 1)

Shifting Focus: From Build to Release

Recall our key distinctions:

- **Build Pipelines (CI):** Focus on code transformation, testing, and artifact production.
- **Release Pipelines (CD):** Focus on taking those artifacts and orchestrating their deployment across environments.

Release Pipeline Components

1. **Artifacts:** The output of your build pipeline – the bits ready for deployment.
2. **Triggers:** What kicks off a release?
   - Automated (a successful build), manual, or scheduled.
3. **Stages:** Logical units representing your environments (Dev, Test, Production…)
4. **Tasks:** Actions within a stage. Think of these as deployment steps. Examples:
   - Azure Web App Deployment
   - Running Database Scripts
   - Custom PowerShell or bash scripts.

Creating Your First Release Pipeline

1. **Navigate to Pipelines (in your Azure DevOps project) -> Releases**.
2. **Click 'New Pipeline'.**
3. **Choose a Template:** For a basic start, select something like 'Azure App Service Deployment'. This gives you a pre-structured foundation.

Stage 1: The 'Dev' Deployment

Let's dissect a simplified example focusing on your initial development environment:

```
trigger: none # Adjust later, for now we'll trigger
manually

stages:
- stage: 'DeployToDev'
  displayName: 'Deploy to Development'

  jobs:
    - job: 'Deploy'
      steps:
      - task: AzureWebAppDeployment@4
        inputs:
          azureSubscription: 'Your Azure
Subscription'
          appType: 'webApp'
          appName: 'your-web-app-name-dev'
          package:
$(Build.ArtifactStagingDirectory)/**/*.zip # Or the
path to your artifact
```

Let's Break It Down

- **stage:** Defines our Dev environment deployment.
- **job:** A collection of tasks that execute together.
- **task:** The AzureWebAppDeployment task is specialized for deploying web applications to Azure.
- **inputs:** We configure the task with details about our Azure subscription, resource names, and the location of our build artifact.

Additional Resources

- **Azure Pipelines Release Tasks:**
  https://docs.microsoft.com/en-us/azure/devops/pipelines/tasks/?view=azure-devops&tabs=yaml
- **Azure Pipelines Stages:**
  https://docs.microsoft.com/en-us/azure/devops/pipelines/process/stages?view=azure-devops

Next Steps

A single-stage deployment is a good start, but the true power of release pipelines comes from multi-stage orchestration and approvals. That's what we'll tackle in Part 2!

Constructing a DevOps Release Pipeline (Part 2)

Scenario: Building Out a Release Flow

Let's imagine a typical path: Dev -> Staging -> Production

Enhancing Your Pipeline

```
trigger: none

stages:
- stage: 'DeployToDev'
  displayName: 'Deploy to Development'
  jobs:
    # ... your Dev Job from Part 1 ...

- stage: 'DeployToStaging'
  displayName: 'Deploy to Staging'
  dependsOn: DeployToDev  # Ensures order
  jobs:
  - deployment: 'Deploy'
    environment: 'Staging'  # Environments are
powerful!
    strategy:
      runOnce:
        deploy:
          steps:
            # ... Similar to Dev, but target your
Staging resources ...

- stage: 'DeployToProd'
  displayName: 'Deploy to Production'
  dependsOn: DeployToStaging
  jobs:
  - deployment: 'Deploy'
    environment: 'Production'
    strategy:
```

```
    runOnce:
      deploy:
        steps:
          - task: ManualIntervention@0 # Approval
gate!
            inputs:
              instructions: 'QA Team: Please
approve for Production'
              # ... more options for timeout,
approvers, etc.
              # ... your production deployment task
here ...
```

Key Additions

- **Stages & Dependencies:** Stages execute in order, controlled by dependsOn.
- **Environments:** Group tasks and settings for different target environments. They offer variables and more (beyond the scope of this chapter).
- **Approvals (`ManualIntervention`):** Pause the pipeline awaiting input from designated individuals or groups.

Triggering the Release

- **Automated from Build:** Configure your build pipeline to trigger this release on completion.
- **Manual Start:** Within Azure Pipelines, create a release manually.

Post-Deployment Tasks

Consider adding these types of tasks after your core deployment steps:

- **Smoke Tests:** Run basic automated tests to check if your deployment broke anything obvious.
- **Notifications:** Send emails or team messages on deployment status.

Additional Resources

- **Azure Pipelines - Approvals:**
  https://docs.microsoft.com/en-us/azure/devops/pipelines/process/approvals
- **Azure Pipelines - Environments:**
  https://docs.microsoft.com/en-us/azure/devops/pipelines/process/environments?view=azure-devops

Next Steps

A multi-stage pipeline with approvals brings you much closer to production-ready automation! Next, we might address common issues you'll encounter in real-world deployments.

Real-World Troubleshooting (Part 1)

Even with the most meticulous planning, unforeseen challenges can arise in Azure Pipelines. Knowing how to effectively troubleshoot and resolve issues is essential for minimizing downtime and ensuring smooth deployments. In this chapter, we'll delve into common Azure Pipeline problems and step-by-step strategies to solve them.

1. Build Pipeline Failures

- **Compilation Errors:**
  - **Check Build Logs:** Start by carefully examining the build logs for specific error messages related to your code.
  - **Dependency Issues:** Ensure all required dependencies are correctly installed and referenced in your project's configuration files.
  - **Incorrect Build Definitions:** Double-check your build definition in the YAML file or classic editor to verify that the build steps and configurations are accurate.
- **Test Failures:**
  - **Test Code Analysis:** Review your test cases to identify flawed logic, incorrect assumptions, or bugs within the tests themselves.
  - **Investigate Intermittent Failures:** If tests pass sometimes and fail other times, focus on possible race conditions or dependencies on external resources that might not always be available.
  - **Optimize Timeouts:** Increase test timeouts if necessary, ensuring your tests have adequate time to run.

2. Deployment Pipeline Failures

- **Incorrect Deployment Target Configuration:**
  - Verify your deployment target settings, including resource groups, names, and locations.
  - Ensure that the specified deployment targets are accessible and running.
- **Authentication and Authorization Issues:**

- ○ Review the credentials used to authenticate with Azure resources. Check if they are valid and have the necessary permissions.
- ○ Address any security policies or firewall restrictions that might block deployment access.
- **Incorrect Deployment Scripts or Tasks:**
  - ○ Closely examine your deployment scripts for typos, syntax errors, or outdated commands.
  - ○ Meticulously check the logic and steps of your custom deployment tasks.

3. General Troubleshooting Strategies

- **Leverage Detailed Logging:** Enable verbose or debug-level logging in your pipelines to extract more granular information about potential problem areas.
- **Isolate the Problem:** If possible, break your pipeline into smaller stages to pinpoint which stage is causing the failure. This can narrow your focus.
- **Check Azure Status:** Visit the Azure status dashboard (https://status.azure.com/) to rule out any platform-wide service disruptions or outages that might be impacting your pipelines.
- **Reproduce the Issue in a Local Environment:** Attempt to recreate the issue locally for faster debugging and experimentation with solutions.
- **Utilize Community Support:** Leverage the Azure DevOps community forums and online resources to find solutions to common problems.

Additional Resources:

- **Azure DevOps Troubleshooting Guide:** https://docs.microsoft.com/en-us/azure/devops/organizations/troubleshoot?view=azure-devops
- **Common Azure Pipeline Errors and Fixes:** https://learn.microsoft.com/en-us/azure/devops/pipelines/troubleshooting/troubleshooting?view=azure-devops
- **Microsoft Q&A Forum** https://learn.microsoft.com/en-us/answers/products/

Important Notes

- **Document Your Troubleshooting Process:** Keep detailed notes on identified errors and the steps taken to resolve them. This will aid in resolving similar issues in the future and build your troubleshooting knowledge base.
- **Consider a Staging Environment:** Implementing a separate staging environment can provide a testbed for resolving issues before they affect production systems.

This chapter sets the foundation for effective troubleshooting. In Part 2, we'll dive into more advanced debugging scenarios and optimization techniques for your pipelines.

Real-World Troubleshooting (Part 2)

In Part 1, we began exploring common Azure Pipeline problems and basic troubleshooting steps. In this chapter, we'll tackle more intricate pipeline issues, delve into advanced debugging scenarios, and optimize pipeline reliability.

1. Advanced Troubleshooting Techniques

- **Leveraging the Pipeline Job Diagnostics:** Under the "Initialize Job" step of the pipeline logs, expand the diagnostics for richer details about the job, agent, environment, and variables. This can reveal subtle configuration mismatches.
- **Debugging with Self-Hosted Agents:** When using self-hosted agents, ensure they have the correct dependencies, tools, and software installed. Run pipelines in debug mode on the agent machines for direct visibility into the execution process.
- **Analyzing Conditional Logic:** Carefully inspect the conditional logic in your pipeline's YAML structure or in classic editor tasks. Small errors in conditions can lead to unexpected behaviors.
- **Inspecting Environment Variables:** Thoroughly examine environment variables for unexpected values or scope limitations. Pay attention to how these variables interact with your pipeline tasks.

2. Common Release Pipeline Issues

- **Approval Gate Failures:**
  - Verify that approvers have the necessary permissions.
  - Ensure that approval timeouts are appropriate to avoid delays.
  - Clearly define approval criteria to prevent confusion.
- **Deployment Target Availability:**
  - Ensure that deployment targets (VMs, web apps, etc.) are in a healthy state and can be reached by the pipeline.
  - Verify firewall rules and any network security configurations that might be blocking access.
- **Task Configuration Errors:**

- ○ Meticulously review environment names, deployment scripts, and task parameters for potential mistakes.
- ○ Test custom tasks in isolation during initial development for faster troubleshooting.

3. Optimizing Pipeline Performance

- **Caching Build Artifacts:** Enable artifact caching to avoid rebuilding components that haven't changed, significantly speeding up subsequent builds.
- **Parallel Jobs:** Where appropriate, split your pipeline into parallel jobs to execute multiple tasks simultaneously, leading to faster completion times.
- **Selective Triggering:** Use branch and path filters to trigger pipelines only when relevant changes occur, optimizing resource usage.
- **Agent Pool Selection:** Choose the correct agent pool (Microsoft-hosted vs. self-hosted) based on performance requirements and project needs.

4. Tooling and Extensions

- **Azure Pipelines Troubleshooting Extension:** Install the official troubleshooter extension (https://marketplace.visualstudio.com/items?itemName=ms-azuredevops.azure-pipelines-troubleshooting) for guided assistance within your Azure DevOps environment.
- **PowerShell Debugging:** Utilize PowerShell's debugging capabilities within your Azure Pipeline tasks for step-by-step troubleshooting and variable inspection.
- **Third-party extensions:** Explore the Azure DevOps marketplace to find specific extensions that can aid with performance monitoring, detailed reporting, and issue tracking.

Additional Resources

- **Detailed Logging Documentation**
  https://learn.microsoft.com/en-us/azure/devops/pipelines/troubleshooting/review-logs?view=azure-devops

- **Self-hosted Agents Guide**
  https://learn.microsoft.com/en-us/azure/devops/pipelines/agents/agents?view=azure-devops
- **Azure DevOps Marketplace**
  https://marketplace.visualstudio.com/azuredevops

Key Reminders

- **Systematic Approach:** Troubleshooting is an iterative process. Remain methodical and analyze information carefully.
- **Seek Assistance:** Don't hesitate to leverage online forums, the Azure DevOps community, and Microsoft support if you encounter particularly complex issues.

By applying these advanced strategies, you'll be well-equipped to resolve pipeline challenges and ensure smooth CI/CD workflows!

Validating Deployments

After a successful code build, it's crucial to guarantee that your deployments function as intended and don't introduce regressions into production environments. A robust deployment validation strategy ensures application quality, minimizes risks, and boosts user satisfaction.

1. Types of Deployment Validation

- **Smoke Tests:** Basic, rapid tests to check if the core functionality of your application is operational after deployment. These confirm that the deployment process itself was successful.
- **Integration Tests:** Verify communication and data exchange between different components and systems of your application after deployment changes.
- **Regression Tests:** Ensure that existing features remain unaltered and behave as expected after code updates to prevent unexpected side-effects from new changes.
- **End-to-end Tests:** Simulate realistic user scenarios and flows through your application's entire user journey in the deployed environment.
- **Performance Tests:** Assess how your application responds under specific load conditions, ensuring it can meet performance targets after code changes.
- **Security Testing:** Perform vulnerability scanning and penetration tests to pinpoint potential security flaws introduced by updates.

2. Strategies for Implementing Deployment Validation

- **Automated Testing within Pipelines:** Incorporate the various testing types as tasks directly within your Azure Pipelines, enabling them to run automatically after a deployment. Here are some tools to consider:
    - **Azure Test Plans Integration:** For manual and automated test case execution. (https://docs.microsoft.com/en-us/azure/devops/test/?view=azure-devops)

- ○ **Unit Test Frameworks:** Such as xUnit, NUnit, MSTest (for C#), or JUnit (for Java).
- ○ **Specialized Tools:** Consider Selenium, Cypress, Appium, and others for functional, UI, and mobile testing.
- **Post-Deployment Validation:**
  - ○ **Canary Deployments:** Release changes to a small subset of users or to a limited set of servers to observe behavior in the production environment.
  - ○ **Blue-Green Deployments:** Deploy a new application version in parallel with the current one, gradually shifting traffic to the new version for seamless cutover.
  - ○ **Feature Flags:** Allow selective activation or deactivation of new features in production for controlled rollout and testing with real users.

3. Monitoring and Logging

- **Utilize Application Insights:** Leverage Application Insights for real-time telemetry, performance metrics, and error reporting on your deployed systems.
  (https://learn.microsoft.com/en-us/azure/azure-monitor/app/app-insights-overview)
- **Centralized Log Aggregation:** Store logs from all deployment targets to aid in troubleshooting and retrospective analysis. Log Analytics is a useful Azure service for this.
  (https://learn.microsoft.com/en-us/azure/azure-monitor/logs/log-analytics-overview)

4. Rollback Strategies

- **Prepare Rollback Mechanisms:** Have pre-tested rollback procedures to quickly revert to a previous working state in case of deployment failures or critical issues.
- **Automatic Rollback Triggering:** Define thresholds for error rates, performance degradation, or user feedback that trigger automatic rollbacks to limit disruptions.

Key Considerations

- **Balancing Thoroughness and Agility:** Design a validation process that's sufficiently rigorous, while retaining the speed benefits of CI/CD practices.
- **Collaboration is Key:** Work closely with developers, testers, and operations teams for a holistic validation approach.

Remember: Deployment validation is an ongoing, iterative process. As your application evolves, continuously refine your tests and validation mechanisms to maintain a smooth user experience.

Streamlining Deployment Automation with YAML Configuration

Why YAML? (A Recap)

- **Declarative:** Describe *what* you want your pipeline to do, not the nitty-gritty steps (YAML handles that).
- **Readable:** Much friendlier than older GUI-based pipeline creation tools.
- **Version Control Friendly:** Your build and release definitions live as code, trackable in your repository.
- **Reusable:** Pipeline elements can be modularized for use across different projects.

Core Structure of a YAML Pipeline

Let's revisit a simple example:

```
trigger:
- main

pool:
 vmImage: 'ubuntu-latest'

steps:
- script: echo Hello, Azure Pipelines!
```

Beyond the Basics

A YAML pipeline offers rich configuration for complex scenarios:

- **Variables:** Define values (target environments, etc.) to reuse within your pipeline, making changes easier.
- **Conditions:** Make your pipeline behave dynamically (e.g., run certain steps only if triggered from a specific branch).
- **Templates:** Create reusable YAML fragments to avoid duplication.

- **Multi-Job & Multi-Stage:** Structure those large release pipelines with dependencies.

Crafting Your YAML

1. **Start Small:** Convert an existing pipeline with the "View YAML" feature in Azure DevOps.
2. **Reference is Your Friend:** Lean on the official documentation for all the possible options.
3. **Schema to the Rescue:** Many IDEs (like VS Code) have extensions for YAML schemas for pipelines, providing autocompletion and error checking.

Example: Parameterizing a Deployment Task

```yaml
variables:
  environmentName: 'Dev'

stages:
- stage: Deploy
  jobs:
  - deployment:
    environment: ${{ variables.environmentName }}
    strategy:
      runOnce:
        deploy:
          steps:
          - task: AzureWebAppDeployment@4
            inputs:
              app-name: 'my-web-app-${{
variables.environmentName }}'
```

Tips

- **Iterate:** You won't get your YAML perfect on the first draft. Test frequently!
- **Linter Tools:** Consider linters for YAML to catch style and basic structural errors.

- **Azure Pipelines Designer:** Sometimes a visual view is helpful, especially when starting out. Azure Pipelines has a designer that can generate basic YAML

Additional Resources

- **Azure Pipelines YAML Schema:**
  https://docs.microsoft.com/en-us/azure/devops/pipelines/yaml-schema
- **YAML Lint (Example Online Tool):**
  https://yamllint.readthedocs.io/en/stable/

Initiating DevOps with CI/CD Pipelines (Part 1)

The Big Picture

CI/CD (Continuous Integration, Continuous Delivery) is at the core of DevOps. Here's the flow:

1. **Code Change:** You (or a teammate) push new code to your repository.
2. **CI Trigger:** This change automatically kicks off a build pipeline.
3. **Build and Test:** Your CI pipeline compiles the code, runs your tests, and produces an artifact.
4. **CD Trigger:** A successful build often triggers your release pipeline.
5. **Automated Deployment:** Your release pipeline orchestrates the deployment of your artifact to Dev (and potentially beyond).

Key Benefits

- **Catch Errors Early:** Automated builds and tests identify issues quickly, preventing them from slipping further down the line.
- **Shorter Feedback Loop:** Developers get near-instant feedback on whether they broke anything.
- **Increased Deployment Velocity:** Releases become routine with less reliance on manual, error-prone processes.
- **Improved Confidence:** With good test coverage, you can trust that your deployments are less likely to fail spectacularly.

First Step: A Solid Build Pipeline

Remember, a CI/CD workflow relies on a reliable build process. If your build is flaky, everything downstream suffers. Ensure your build pipeline from previous chapters is robust.

Connecting CI Triggers

In Azure Pipelines, configure your build pipeline's settings:

- **Trigger Type:** Common options include:

- Automatic (On commits to specified branches)
- Scheduled (run on a regular basis, e.g., nightly)
- **Branch Filters:** Builds might trigger only on changes to your 'main' branch, or specific feature branches.

Setting up a Release Trigger

Most likely, a successful build is what you want to deploy:

1. In your release pipeline, go to its settings.
2. Add an artifact and select the build pipeline you just configured as the source.
3. Enable the Continuous Deployment trigger (looks like a lightning bolt) .
4. You can add branch filters (to only deploy from certain branches) and other pre-deployment conditions here.

Additional Resources

- **CI/CD Concepts in Azure DevOps:**
  https://docs.microsoft.com/en-us/azure/devops/pipelines/get-started/key-pipelines-concepts?view=azure-devops
- **Azure Pipelines Triggers:**
  https://docs.microsoft.com/en-us/azure/devops/pipelines/build/triggers

Next Steps

With CI/CD connected, you're truly automating deployment! In Part 2, we'll focus on deploying to an actual environment using Azure Pipelines features and tasks.

Initiating DevOps with CI/CD Pipelines (Part 2)

Scenario: Deploying a Web App

Let's assume you have a simple Azure Web App service ready as your deployment target. We'll focus on the mechanics of getting your code there using Azure Pipelines.

Enhancing Your Release Pipeline

Recall the basic structure from Part 1. We'll focus on a 'Deploy to Dev' stage:

```
stages:
- stage: DeployToDev
  jobs:
    - deployment: Deploy
      environment: Dev
      strategy:
        runOnce:
          deploy:
            steps:
              - task: AzureWebAppDeployment@4
                inputs:
                  azureSubscription: 'Your Azure
Subscription'
                  appType: 'webApp'
                  appName: 'your-web-app-name-dev'
                  package:
$(Build.ArtifactStagingDirectory)/**/*.zip
```

Important Notes

- **Service Connections:** Your pipeline needs authorization to interact with Azure resources. Within Azure DevOps, set up a 'Service Connection' to your Azure subscription.

- **Adapt to Your Tech:** The `AzureWebAppDeployment@4` task is specific to web apps. Azure Pipelines has tasks for databases, virtual machines, containers, and more!

Deployment Strategies

As your process matures, consider strategies like these (often handled within your deployment tasks):

- **Blue-Green:** Deploy to a parallel environment, switch over traffic for minimal downtime.
- **Canary:** Gradually route a percentage of real traffic to the new version, validating before a full rollout.
- **Rolling:** Incremental updates across instances to avoid complete outages.

Test and Iterate

1. **Make a Safe Change:** Modify a webpage to have something obvious like "CI/CD Test Success!"
2. **Commit & Push:** Trigger your pipeline!
3. **Behold:** Check your dev environment; changes should be deployed.

Beyond the Basics

A real-world pipeline might include:

- **Pre-Deployment Approvals:** Gates for pausing deployment awaiting manual sign-off.
- **Smoke Test Steps:** Automated tests to verify basic functionality post-deployment.
- **Notifications:** Integrations with Teams, Slack, etc., to keep your team informed.

Additional Resources

- **Azure Pipelines Deployment Strategies:**
  https://docs.microsoft.com/en-us/azure/devops/pipelines/release/deployment-jobs?view=azure-devops

- **Azure DevOps Environments:**
  https://docs.microsoft.com/en-us/azure/devops/pipelines/process/environments?view=azure-devops&tabs=yaml

Crafting Azure Deployment Pipelines from Your IDE (Part 1)

Why Use an IDE?

- **Seamless Workflow** Create and modify pipelines without leaving your code editor.
- **Assisted Authoring** Extensions provide autocomplete, and validation for YAML structure.
- **Integrated Experience:** Debug your code and your pipeline definition in one place.

Prerequisites

1. **Supported IDE:** Popular choices include:
   - Visual Studio Code (we'll focus on this)
   - Visual Studio
2. **Azure Pipelines Extension:** Install the official extension from your IDE's marketplace
3. **Azure DevOps Connection:** The extension often guides you to connect your IDE to your Azure DevOps organization.

Creating Your First Pipeline from the IDE

1. **Azure Pipelines View:** Most extensions add a dedicated view within your IDE to manage pipelines.
2. **"New Pipeline" Option:** This typically starts a wizard-like process.
3. **Basics:** You'll select:
   - Where your code is (Azure Repos Git, GitHub…)
   - The type of technology you're building (Node.js, .NET, etc.).
4. **Starter Template:** The extension usually offers a template matching your project. This gives you a solid YAML foundation.
5. **Save and Push:** Commit your generated pipeline YAML file to your repo!

Example Workflow (VS Code)

1. Open the Azure Pipelines view in VS Code.
2. 'Create a new pipeline'

3. Select Azure Repos Git, your repository and branch.
4. Choose 'Node.js' as an example.
5. Customize the generated YAML if needed.
6. Save the pipeline, commit, and push to your repository to trigger it.

Additional Notes

- **Not Just Creation:** The extension often lets you view existing pipelines, their run history, etc.
- **Inline Editing:** Some extensions allow editing pipelines alongside your code in a split-view.

Additional Resources

- **Azure Pipelines Extension for VS Code Documentation:** https://marketplace.visualstudio.com/items?itemName=ms-azure-devops.azure-pipelines

Next Steps

IDE integration makes tweaking your pipelines much more convenient. In Part 2, we'll dive into advanced editing and how to manage complex deployment stages from within your editor.

Crafting Azure Deployment Pipelines from Your IDE (Part 2)

Editing Existing Pipelines

Often, you'll modify an existing pipeline and IDE extensions help immensely:

- **Visual Representation:** Some extensions offer a way to visualize your pipeline's stages and tasks, making it easier to grasp complex flows.
- **Autocomplete & Validation:** As you type YAML, you get suggestions for task names, parameters, and valid values. This catches potential errors early.
- **Reference Docs:** Access task documentation directly within your IDE, speeding up adding or tweaking tasks.

Debugging Your Pipeline

When your pipeline misbehaves, the IDE can help:

- **Run History:** View past executions, their status, and logs, all without leaving your code editor.
- **Direct Log Access:** Click into a failed step for its detailed output.
- **Debug Mode (Potentially):** Some extensions might allow setting breakpoints within your YAML pipeline definition for step-by-step investigation.

Multi-Stage Workflows

Let's extend our deployment example from Part 1 with a 'Staging' environment:

```
# ... your existing build job ...

stages:
- stage: DeployToDev
  # ... your existing Dev deployment ...
```

```
- stage: DeployToStaging
  dependsOn: DeployToDev
  jobs:
  - deployment: Deploy
    environment: Staging
    strategy:
      runOnce:
        deploy:
          steps:
            # Deployment task for Staging (adjust as
needed)
```

Managing Variables

IDE extensions usually provide a smoother experience for working with pipeline variables:

- **Dedicated View:** A consolidated list of variables used within your pipeline.
- **Scoped Variables:** Define variables for specific stages or the entire pipeline.
- **Secrets Integration:** Link to Azure Key Vault for sensitive data.

Section 5:
Enhancing Quality with Test Plans and Extensions

Navigating Azure Test Plans: A Comprehensive Introduction

Why Test Plans Matter

- **Beyond Unit Tests:** While unit tests are vital, Azure Test Plans orchestrate a broader variety of testing.
- **Organized Execution:** Ensure important test scenarios are covered and results are tracked methodically.
- **Centralized View:** Gain a consolidated perspective on quality across your project, not scattered across tools.
- **Collaborative:** Assign tests, track progress, and share results with your team.

Core Concepts

- **Test Plan:** The overarching container that groups your tests. A project may have multiple Test Plans.
- **Test Suite:** A way to organize tests within a Test Plan. Suites can be hierarchical (Static, Regression, etc.).
- **Test Case:** An individual test with:
  - Steps (Instructions for a tester)
  - Expected Results
  - Associated work items in Azure Boards (bug tracking, etc.)
- **Test Configurations:** Allow defining variations of a test case (different browsers, operating systems, etc.)

Types of Testing

Azure Test Plans supports:

- **Manual Testing:** Structured instructions for human testers to execute.
- **Automated Testing:** Integration with frameworks like Selenium, enabling you to include automated UI tests, load tests, etc., as part of your plan.

Into the Azure DevOps Interface

You'll find Azure Test Plans withing your project, usually under the 'Test Plans' tab. Here, you can:

- **Create Test Suites and Cases**
- **Assign Testers**
- **Run Tests:** The Test Runner lets testers execute test cases step-by-step, marking results, and capturing screenshots.
- **Charts & Reporting:** Track test run status, outcomes over time, etc.

Example: Testing a Website

You might have a Test Suite for 'Login Functionality' with Test Cases like:

- "Successful login with valid credentials"
- "Unsuccessful login with incorrect password"
- "Login with two-factor authentication enabled"

Additional Resources

- **Azure Test Plans Documentation:**
  https://docs.microsoft.com/en-us/azure/devops/test/?view=azure-devops
- **Using Test Plans for Manual Testing:**
  https://learn.microsoft.com/en-us/azure/devops/test/manual-test-overview?view=azure-devops

Next Steps: A solid testing foundation involves a mix of test types. In upcoming chapters, we'll explore different testing methodologies and how they fit within your Azure DevOps workflow.

Exploring Testing Methodologies (Part 1)

The Importance of Methodology

Software testing isn't just about finding bugs. Methodical approaches help you:

- **Prioritize:** Decide where to focus testing efforts, maximizing the value of your time.
- **Organize:** Structured testing leads to replicable results and easier tracking.
- **Communicate:** A shared language around testing facilitates discussions within your team.

Part 1: The Fundamentals

Let's introduce some core methodologies and when they are commonly used:

- **Unit Testing:**
  - Focus: Testing the smallest isolatable parts of your code (functions, classes).
  - Advantages: Fast execution, pinpoint errors early, often heavily automated.
  - Best For: Foundation of your test pyramid, vital for any size of project.
- **Integration Testing:**
  - Focus: How different components of your system interact (e.g., your frontend talking to a database).
  - Advantages: Catches issues in data flow and component communication.
  - Best For: Once you have working modules, integration tests verify they play well together.
- **Functional Testing:**
  - Focus: Testing against the software's requirements from a user perspective (Does clicking this button do what it's supposed to?)
  - Advantages: Catches errors in actual user experiences.

- Best For: Every project needs this, often as a mix of manual and automated tests.
  - **End-to-End Testing:**
    - Focus: Simulating a complete user journey through your system (login -> search -> checkout).
    - Advantages: Assesses the big picture – are core user flows working?
    - Best For: Critical scenarios, often with a higher portion of manual tests due to complexity

Black Box vs. White Box Testing

You'll often hear this categorization:

- **Black Box:** Tests the software without the tester knowing its internal structure. Focus is on inputs and expected outputs.
- **White Box:** The tester has knowledge of the codebase. Tests might be designed with specific code paths in mind.

Example: A Quiz Game

- Unit Tests: "Does the score calculate correctly given a specific block combination?"
- Integration Tests: "Does saving a high score actually update the database?"
- Functional Tests: "Can the user navigate through the game menus successfully?"
- End-to-End Test: "Can a user start a new game, play a round, and see their score on the leaderboard?"

Additional Resources

- **Types of Software Testing:**
  https://www.ministryoftesting.com/dojo/lessons/an-introduction-to-software-testing

Next Steps: In Part 2, we'll dive into more specialized methodologies like performance testing, and how to map different testing types to the stages of your CI/CD pipeline.

Exploring Testing Methodologies (Part 2)

Beyond the Basics

Let's delve into a few more common testing types:

- **Performance Testing:**
    - Focus: How well does your system handle load? Can it serve the expected number of users without slowing down?
    - Types: Load tests (many users), stress tests (system under extreme pressure), spike tests (sudden bursts of traffic).
    - Best For: Applications with significant traffic expectations.
- **Security Testing:**
    - Focus: Finding vulnerabilities before the bad guys do (e.g., SQL injection, unhandled access, etc.)
    - Types: Penetration testing, vulnerability scans… this is a vast and specialized field
    - Best For: Apps handling sensitive data, or those with strict compliance requirements.
- **Regression Testing:**
    - Focus: Ensuring that changes don't break existing functionality.
    - Advantages: Vital safety net as your project grows!
    - Best For: A core part of any ongoing project, requires a mix of automation and manual checks.

The Testing Pyramid

You'll often see testing visualized as a pyramid:

- **Base: Unit Tests** (Fast, numerous)
- **Middle: Integration Tests**
- **Top: Functional, End-to-End** (Slower, fewer)

This emphasizes the ideal balance: Lots of automated unit tests for fast feedback, and increasingly fewer (and slower) tests as we go up towards user-centric scenarios.

Testing Within Your CI/CD Pipeline

- **Unit Tests:** Should run as part of your CI build. Failing these should often block a deployment.
- **Integration Tests:** May run in CI or as a first step in your release pipeline. Frequency depends on speed of execution.
- **Smoke Tests:** A quick set of core functional tests to verify deployment health, post-deploy.
- **Longer Tests:** Performance, security, *some* end-to-end might be on schedules (nightly) or gated by approval in your release pipeline.

An Example Pipeline for a Game

1. **CI on Commit:** Unit tests run, must pass.
2. **Deployment to Dev:** Integration tests, smoke tests.
3. **Approval for Staging:** Run a load test for basic performance validation.
4. **Production Readiness:** Vulnerability scan, limited end-to-end suite.

Additional Resources

- **Test Automation with Azure DevOps:** Azure Pipelines can run various test types
  https://docs.microsoft.com/en-us/azure/devops/test/?view=azure-devops
- **Visual Studio Testing Tools:**
  https://docs.microsoft.com/en-us/visualstudio/test/?view=vs-2022

Next Steps

Knowing your testing options is the first step. Next, we'll explore the practical side: how to design effective manual test plans within tools like Azure Test Plans.

Designing Manual Test Plans (Part 1)

Why Manual Tests Still Matter

- **True User Perspective:** Automated tests are great, but they can't fully mimic a human's thought process and interactions.
- **Exploratory:** Good testers uncover unexpected behaviors that automated scripts wouldn't think about.
- **Usability Focus:** Manual tests can assess whether an interface is intuitive, not just functionally correct.

Components of a Manual Test Case

Within Azure Test Plans, and most test management tools, you'll find a structure like this:

- **Title:** Descriptive name for the test.
- **Steps:** Clear, numbered instructions for what the tester should do, and in what order.
- **Expected Result:** The exact outcome to validate, at each step.
- **Associated Work Items:** Links to user stories, bug reports in Azure Boards, etc. This creates traceability.
- **Data:** If the test needs specific input (user accounts, etc.) it's defined here.

Test Plan Organization

- **Test Suites:** Group your test cases logically ("Login Tests", "Checkout Flow Tests", etc.)
- **Hierarchical Suites:** Suites can be nested within each other for organization in large projects.
- **Test Configurations:** Handle testing the same scenario on different environments (Windows, macOS, various browsers…)

Example: 'New Game' Test Case

- **Title:** New Game Functionality
- **Steps:**
    1. Navigate to the Game's main page.
    2. Click the "New Game" button.

3. Verify a game board is displayed.
4. Verify the score starts at 0.

- **Expected Result:** At each step, the described UI element is present and in the correct state.

Tips for Effective Plans

- **Clarity is King:** Your tester should need no further explanation than what's written in the case.
- **Think 'Edge Cases':** Don't just test the happy path! What if the user does things in a strange order, or enters odd data?
- **Specificity:** "The page looks right" is bad. "The success message is green and says 'Order Complete'" is good.
- **Screenshots:** Encourage testers to capture evidence, especially for failures.

Additional Resources

- **Azure Test Plans: Creating Test Cases:**
  https://docs.microsoft.com/en-us/azure/devops/test/author-test-plans?view=azure-devops

Next Steps

A written plan is vital, but how testers execute matters! In Part 2, we'll cover test runs, reporting results, and integrating this smoothly into your development workflow within Azure DevOps.

Designing Manual Test Plans (Part 2)

Executing Test Runs

Azure Test Plans provides a dedicated Test Runner interface. Here's a more in-depth look at the process:

1. **Assign Testers:** Choose who's responsible for a given Test Suite or individual cases. Consider specialization – some testers might be better at exploratory testing, while others meticulously work through detailed steps.
2. **Start a Run:** A tester picks up a Test Case, starting a new run. They're not just robots though: think of skilled testers as extensions of your development team, bringing valuable critical thinking to the process.
3. **Step-by-Step:** While following instructions, the tester constantly looks for inconsistencies or outright unexpected behavior. This is where truly valuable bugs surface!
4. **Outcomes:** Tests might result in a simple Pass/Fail, or more nuanced outcomes like "Partially Passed" with tester notes explaining the issue.
5. **Evidence:** Beyond screenshots, testers might capture screen recordings (helpful for complex interactions), or even log files generated by the application during the test.

Tracking Results

- **Individual Runs:** Detailed records of test executions are key to resolving issues. Did a test that previously failed suddenly succeed? It might point to a flaky test, or a fix that needs further verification.
- **Aggregated in Azure Test Plans:** Charts, reports, and filtering provide a high-level picture of your project's quality. Are certain modules consistently problematic? Perhaps they require refactoring or additional automated tests for a tighter feedback cycle.

Linking Bugs to Tests

1. **Fail a Test:** While failing a test step, testers have streamlined options like "Create Bug" or "Link to Existing Bug" for recurring issues.
2. **Information Transfer:** Test Case details, screenshots, and any tester observations become the foundation of the bug report, saving time and minimizing miscommunication.
3. **Traceability:** This bi-directional linking (requirements -> test case -> bugs, but also bug -> failed cases) is invaluable for both current troubleshooting and future regression prevention.

Iterating on Your Test Plan

- **Refinement:** Treat your tests as a living part of your codebase. Prioritize updating tests alongside feature development to avoid discrepancies.
- **New Bugs as Test Cases:** Critical or elusive bugs, once fixed, are prime candidates for new test cases. This proactively bakes quality into the process.
- **Prioritization:** Balance comprehensive testing with agility. Focus on frequently executed tests for critical functionality, while scheduling longer, exploratory suites less often.

Test Runs, CI/CD and Beyond

- **Gating Deployments:** Failing critical tests should act as safeguards, potentially even pausing or rolling back a problematic release.
- **Smoke Test Phase:** Post-deployment, ensure basic health and sanity with 'smoke' tests, where human judgment offers an extra layer of confidence.
- **Exploratory After the Fact:** Allow testers the creative freedom to explore new features or intentionally 'break' the system, often uncovering surprising issues.
- **Feedback for the Future:** Test results aren't just about the present. They fuel planning, indicating where code might need extra attention or where a feature might be inherently prone to errors.

Additional Resources

- **Azure Test Plans: Execute tests:**
  https://docs.microsoft.com/en-us/azure/devops/test/run-tests?view=azure-devops&tabs=browser
- **The Value of Exploratory Testing:**
  https://www.ministryoftesting.com/dojo/lessons/the-value-of-exploratory-testing

Next Steps

Manual tests offer a human touch that automated tests can't replicate. Next, let's tackle load testing: the art of simulating real-world traffic to proactively find your system's breaking points.

Conducting URL Load Tests: Evaluating Performance with Precision

Why Load Testing Matters

- **Functionality is Not Enough:** Even a perfectly coded application can buckle if it isn't designed to scale. Load testing exposes those hidden weaknesses.
- **Beyond the Breaking Point:** Don't just test if your app fails, but how it fails. Does it gradually slow down? Do specific features become agonizing to use before a total crash? This information is crucial for optimization.
- **Data-Driven Decisions:** Load testing arms you with hard data to justify infrastructure investments. Instead of guessing how many servers you need, you can back up your requirements with concrete test results.
- **Confidence Builder:** A successful load test instills confidence that your application can weather the traffic spikes that come with launches, promotions, or viral events.

Key Concepts (Metrics)

- **Virtual Users:** Software entities that simulate the actions of real users, putting your system under stress.
- **Requests per Second (RPS):** The raw measure of how much traffic your application can handle at a given moment.
- **Response Time:** How quickly your system responds to individual requests under load. This metric directly impacts user experience and should remain within acceptable bounds.
- **Error Rate:** As load ramps up, do errors start to appear? This is a sign of components reaching their limits.
- **Percentiles:** Focus on the 95th or 99th percentile response time. This ensures a good experience for the vast majority of your users, even those experiencing the longest wait times.

Tools of the Trade

Let's delve a little deeper into some popular options:

- **Azure Load Testing (Preview):** A powerful managed service seamlessly integrated into Azure DevOps. Its ease of use makes it an excellent choice if you're primarily within the Azure ecosystem.
- **k6:** This open-source tool offers tremendous flexibility, using JavaScript for test scripting. If your team is already comfortable with JavaScript, k6 allows for highly customized test scenarios.
- **JMeter:** A time-tested open-source workhorse with a GUI-driven approach. It might have a slight learning curve, but offers a wide breadth of features for complex test designs.

Load Testing Strategies

- **Smoke Tests:** Simple tests integrated into CI/CD for a quick sanity check after deployments. "Can the system handle a baseline level of traffic?"
- **Stress Tests:** Pushing your system towards its limits to identify breaking points and understand its failure modes.
- **Spike Tests:** Simulating sudden bursts of traffic, akin to a flash sale or a social media buzz.
- **Endurance Tests:** Running tests over extended periods to uncover memory leaks or gradual performance degradation that shorter tests might miss.

Example: Quiz Game at Scale

- **Test Targets:** Consider testing both your frontend (how does rendering many game boards at once impact the browser?) and your backend APIs for handling score submission, leaderboard updates, etc.
- **Gradual Ramp Up:** Real-world traffic rarely jumps from zero to maximum instantly. Simulate a realistic traffic buildup.
- **Visualizations Matter:** Tools like k6 or JMeter provide real-time graphs during tests, allowing you to pinpoint the exact moment performance starts to degrade.

Additional Resources

- **Azure Load Testing Documentation:**
  https://docs.microsoft.com/en-us/azure/devops/test/load-test/overview?view=azure-devops
- **k6.io (Includes detailed examples):** https://k6.io/
- **JMeter Tutorial:** https://www.guru99.com/jmeter-tutorials.html

Next Steps

Load testing provides preventive medicine for your app. Next, we'll tackle real-time monitoring with tools like Application Insights, ensuring you know what's happening within your production environment.

Section 6:
Continuous Monitoring and Optimization

Introduction to Continuous Monitoring: Understanding the Importance

The Shift: From Reactive to Proactive

- **Old Times:** You found out about problems when customers complained, or worse, when the whole system went down in flames.
- **Continuous Monitoring:** Provides a real-time pulse of your application's health and behavior, allowing you to fix issues…sometimes even before users notice them.

Why Continuous Monitoring Is Key for DevOps

- **Deployment Confidence:** If you know something is broken the instant it goes live, you can rapidly roll back or mitigate. This enables faster iteration and bolder releases.
- **Uncovering the Unseen:** Monitoring goes beyond simple 'up or down' checks. It reveals slowdowns, memory leaks, or odd error patterns that might fly under the radar of regular testing.
- **The Basis for Everything:** You can't optimize what you can't measure. Data provided by monitoring drives informed decisions about scaling, improvements, and even informs the prioritization of future development.
- **Culture Shift:** A well-monitored system breeds a proactive team culture. The focus moves from firefighting towards continuous improvement.

Pillars of Continuous Monitoring

Let's break down the core components of what most monitoring solutions offer:

- **Metrics:** Numeric data like response times, CPU usage, memory consumption, error rates…these are the basic building blocks.
- **Logs:** Detailed records of events within your applications and infrastructure. Invaluable when troubleshooting specific issues, tracing transactions, or analyzing long-term trends.
- **Alerts:** Configurable rules that trigger notifications when metrics cross thresholds, or specific entries appear in your logs (e.g., a spike in "500 Internal Server Error" messages).
- **Visualization (Dashboards):** Custom dashboards turn raw data into meaningful, at-a-glance views of your system's health. Charts, graphs, and status indicators make the information digestible.

Example: Monitoring a Hypothetical Game

You'd want to monitor things like:

- **Server Health:** Are the servers running out of disk space, RAM, etc.? (Basic infrastructure health)
- **API Responsiveness:** How quickly does the backend respond to leaderboard updates, player move submissions, etc.?
- **Error Rates:** Are client-side errors (in player's browsers) increasing due to a buggy release?
- **User Volume:** Monitoring active users helps you plan for scaling your infrastructure needs.

Integrating Monitoring into Your Workflow

- **Part of the Pipeline:** Deployment pipelines might include steps to alert if critical health metrics degrade after pushing new code.
- **Feedback into Azure Boards:** Alerts can automatically create work items on your board, streamlining the resolution process.
- **Don't Monitor in Isolation:** Tie insights from monitoring back to individual code changes, releases, and feature flags to better understand the impact of your work.

Additional Resources

- **Types of Monitoring:**
  https://www.datadoghq.com/blog/monitoring-101-types-of-monitoring/
- **Monitoring vs. Observability:**
  https://newrelic.com/blog/what-is-observability

Implementing Application Insights for Real-Time Monitoring

What is Application Insights?

- **Managed Service:** A core part of the Azure platform designed specifically for application monitoring.
- **Data Powerhouse:** Captures telemetry (data) about your application, including metrics, logs, request traces, exceptions, and even custom events.
- **Integrations:** Works seamlessly with .NET Core, Java, Node.js apps, and even JavaScript running on the client-side (users' browsers).

Why You Should Care

Application Insights will give you the ability to:

- **Live Metrics:** See how many users are active right now, live request success/failure rates, etc.
- **Powerful Queries:** Slice and dice data to pinpoint issues by time range, browser, location… virtually any dimension.
- **Dependency Mapping:** Understand if your app is slow because of sluggish database calls, or an external API you rely on.
- **Proactive Alerting:** Get notified immediately of unusual error rates or performance dips.

Setting up Application Insights (Basic)

1. **Azure Portal:** Within your Azure subscription, create an Application Insights resource.
2. **Instrumentation Key:** This unique key identifies your app's data stream to Application Insights.
3. **Integrate with Your Code:**
   - **.NET Core:** Install NuGet Package: Microsoft.ApplicationInsights.AspNetCore
   - **Node.js:** Install NPM Package: @microsoft/applicationinsights-web

∘ **Others:** Check Application Insights docs for language-specific guidance

What You Get Out of the Box

- **Requests:** How many, how fast, any failures
- **Dependencies:** Calls to databases, REST APIs, etc., and their timing.
- **Exceptions:** Both server-side and client-side if you instrument your frontend.
- **Page Views:** Useful for tracking user journeys within single-page web applications.
- **User/Session Counts:** Understand the scale at which your app is used.

Example: Enhancing the Game

Let's say you've built a Game with an ASP.NET Core backend:

1. **Add Application Insights to your backend project.**
2. **Add client-side (JavaScript) instrumentation to your game's frontend.**
3. **Deploy and observe!** Within minutes, data starts flowing into Azure.

Key Dashboards & Views

- **Live Metrics:** Real-time, customizable telemetry visualization.
- **Application Map:** Automatically discovers and maps relationships between your app components.
- **Failures:** Investigate exceptions, drill down to raw logs for context.

Additional Resources

- **Official Application Insights Documentation:** https://docs.microsoft.com/azure/azure-monitor/app/app-insights-overview

Next Steps: Monitoring is just the beginning! Next, we'll look at configuring smart alerts to turn this wealth of data into actionable notifications to keep your applications running smoothly.

Setting Up Alerts and Notifications for Proactive Monitoring

Why Alerts Matter

- **Don't Be the Last to Know:** Get notified before customers are inconvenienced by major issues.
- **The Faster, the Better:** Early warning means faster fixes, and less time spent under production fire.
- **Tailored to Your Needs:** From simple threshold alerts to complex multi-condition scenarios, define what constitutes 'something is wrong' for your specific application.
- **Beyond Just Email:** Integrate alerts with collaboration tools to ensure your team sees them where they already work.

Types of Alerts in Azure

Let's look at the main categories:

- **Metric Alerts:** The most common type. "If server response time exceeds 1 second for 5 minutes, notify me."
- **Log Search Alerts:** Based on the powerful Kusto Query Language within Application Insights and Log Analytics. Example: "If more than 10 'Payment Failed' entries appear in my logs in an hour…"
- **Availability Tests:** Actively probe your website or API endpoints from various geographic regions. If it fails to respond correctly, you'll know.
- **Near-Real-Time Alerts:** Special types of metric alerts that fire within seconds of an issue arising, crucial for super time-sensitive scenarios.

Setting up an Alert (Example)

Let's walk through a metric alert for a quiz game:

1. **In Azure Portal:** Go to your Application Insights resource.
2. **"Alerts" Section:** Select "Add Alert"

3. **Scope:** Choose the metric to monitor (e.g., "Server Response Time")
4. **Condition:** Set a threshold ("Average" > "1.5 seconds")
5. **Period:** Over what time window to evaluate the rule ("Over the last 5 minutes")
6. **Action Group:** This is KEY (create one if you haven't already). Action Groups define *what actually happens* when the alert triggers:
    - **Send an Email**
    - **SMS message**
    - Webhook for custom integrations (Slack, Teams, PagerDuty, etc.)

Smart Alerting Practices

- **Tier Alerts:** Have different severity levels to avoid constant noise. A slightly elevated error rate might just be a 'Warning' email, while a critical outage should trigger the full alarm barrage.
- **Testing Your Alerts:** Deliberately trigger them in a test environment to ensure the right actions and notifications happen.
- **Don't Ignore Them:** Alerts that are ignored breed contempt for the system itself. Either tune thresholds to avoid false alarms, or be truly ready to respond!

Integrating with the Bigger Picture

- **Azure Boards:** Consider creating work items for certain types of alerts to track their resolution.
- **Deployment Pipeline:** Potentially pause rollouts if critical alerts fire during or shortly after a new deployment.
- **Alert Suppression:** If you have scheduled maintenance, consider temporarily suppressing alerts to avoid false alarms.

Additional Resources

- **Azure Alerts Overview:** https://docs.microsoft.com/azure/azure-monitor/alerts/alerts-overview

- **Working with Action Groups:**
  https://docs.microsoft.com/en-us/azure/azure-monitor/alerts/action-groups

Next Steps

With a robust alerting system in place, let's now look at how to utilize these insights, along with raw logs, to pinpoint the root causes of performance issues within your code.

Analyzing Application Performance: Identifying Bottlenecks and Improvements

The Investigative Mindset

- **Correlation is Key:** Alerts tell you *that* something is wrong. Now, we figure out *why*. Look for corresponding spikes in error rates, unusual log entries, or even infrastructure resource usage around the time performance degrades.
- **Ask Questions:** "Did this slow-down start after our last deploy? Is it affecting all users, or users in a specific location? Does it happen only at certain times of day?"
- **Baseline is Your Friend:** It's hard to know what's "slow" without a sense of what's normal for your application. Averages over time are helpful in understanding expected performance.

Tools of the Trade

Let's focus on Application Insights, but other monitoring services offer similar capabilities:

- **Performance Profiler:** Samples your running app code, giving you a breakdown of where the time is spent. This is invaluable for pinpointing slow functions or suboptimal database queries.
- **Transaction Search:** Drill down into individual requests. "Show me the 50 slowest user requests in the past hour, and their detailed traces." This lets you isolate problematic code paths.
- **Application Map:** Great for visualizing how requests flow through different parts of your system. Bottlenecks often become visually obvious as you see where calls to certain components stack up.

Example: What's Holding it Back?

1. **Notice the Alert:** Your 'Server Response Time' alert is firing repeatedly.
2. **Examine Traces:** Dig into failed/slow traces around those alerts. Do certain API endpoints seem to be the culprit?

3. **Profile:** If possible, run the profiler on your backend. This might uncover issues like a poorly written database query that gets exponentially slower as your player base grows.
4. **Dependency Analysis:** Does that slow API rely on an external system that's also slowing down? The Application Map is great for this.

Beyond the Obvious

- **Client-Side Woes:** Is the issue actually too much JavaScript processing in players' browsers? Application Insights can track that too.
- **Infrastructure Limits:** Sometimes, the app is fine, but your servers are hitting CPU or database connection limits. Correlate your app metrics with infrastructure metrics provided by Azure Monitor.
- **Death by a Thousand Cuts:** Small inefficiencies, when compounded under heavy load, can cause noticeable delays.

Taking Action

- **Code Fixes:** Optimize those slow functions and queries.
- **Caching:** Introduce caching layers to reduce database hits or redundant calculations.
- **Scaling Up:** If the issue is resource starvation, consider upgrading your database tier or adding server instances.
- **Scaling Out:** For truly high-traffic apps, more complex architectures might be the solution (load balancers, message queues, etc.)

Additional Resources

- **Application Insights Profiler:** https://docs.microsoft.com/en-us/azure/azure-monitor/app/profiler-overview
- **Distributed Tracing for Microservices:** https://opentelemetry.io/

Next Steps: Sometimes the raw data isn't enough. Next, we'll look at Azure Log Analytics, where powerful queries help analyze logs for troubleshooting and identifying long-term trends.

Leveraging Log Analytics for Deep Insights and Troubleshooting

Log Analytics: What is It?

- **Centralized Log Store:** A massively scalable repository within Azure where you can send logs from various sources: application logs, infrastructure logs, Azure service logs, and more.
- **Kusto Query Language (KQL):** A powerful language designed for slicing and dicing through enormous datasets efficiently. Think of it like SQL, but tailored for log exploration.

Why Log Analytics Augments Monitoring

- **Beyond Metrics:** Application Insights provides excellent pre-aggregated metrics, but sometimes you need the raw, verbose logs to pinpoint a specific error's cause.
- **Trends Over Time:** Analyze long-term patterns. "Are database query times gradually getting worse across all our servers?"
- **Correlation Central:** Combine data from diverse sources. See if network infrastructure events correspond to spikes in application errors within the same timeframe.

Getting Data into Log Analytics

Azure makes this easy! Here are a few common avenues:

- **Application Insights:** There's built-in integration to forward logs automatically.
- **Azure VMs:** Agents can be installed to collect OS-level logs, system events, etc.
- **Custom Sources:** There's an API to send logs from virtually anywhere, giving you immense flexibility.

Scenario: Troubleshooting a Fleeting Bug in our Hypothetical Game

1. **Notice Unusual Errors:** Your alerts occasionally catch "Payment Gateway Timeout" errors, but they're intermittent.
2. **Search in Logs:** Craft a Kusto query:

```
traces
| where message contains "Payment Gateway" and
severityLevel >= 3
| project timestamp, message
```

3. **Analyze Results:** Are there patterns? Do timeouts happen for specific users, or during high traffic periods? Look for clues in the log entries themselves.
4. **Refine Queries:** KQL lets you summarize, count, and visualize results for easier discovery.

Kusto Query Language Basics

- **Table-Centric:** Think of your data as different tables that can be filtered and joined together.
- **Pipelines:** Use the pipe character (|) to chain commands: `TableName | where Condition | summarize CountOfErrors = count()`
- **Documentation is Your Friend:** There are countless operators and functions for extracting data as needed.

Additional Resources

- **Kusto Query Language (KQL) Documentation:** https://docs.microsoft.com/en-us/azure/data-explorer/kusto/query/
- **Log Analytics Workspaces:** https://docs.microsoft.com/en-us/azure/azure-monitor/logs/data-platform-logs

Next Steps

A healthy DevOps pipeline isn't just about keeping things running, but also about ensuring the highest level of security for your applications. Next, let's explore how to bake security practices into each stage of your development process.

Implementing Security Best Practices in Your DevOps Pipeline

Why "Shift Left" with Security Matters

- **Traditional Thinking:** Security used to be an afterthought tacked onto the end of a project.
- **DevSecOps:** Embedding security concerns into every stage of development leads to more robust software, and catches vulnerabilities *before* they reach production.
- **Cost-Effective:** Finding a critical flaw early is orders of magnitude cheaper than dealing with a breach after your app is deployed.

Key Areas to Secure

Let's look at these through the lens of your DevOps process:

1. **Source Code:**
   - **Vulnerability Scans:** Tools to detect use of libraries with known flaws (e.g., outdated versions of common components).
   - **Secret Scanning:** Prevent accidental committing of API keys, database passwords, etc., into your repositories.
   - **Branch Permissions:** Strict controls on who can merge into sensitive branches, especially the main line of development.
2. **Build Pipeline:**
   - **Hardened Build Servers:** Keep them patched, with minimal software to reduce attack surface.
   - **Artifact Signing:** Ensure what you deploy is exactly what you built, preventing tampering.
3. **Environments:**
   - **Principle of Least Privilege:** Components of your app should have only the bare minimum permissions they need, even within your infrastructure.
   - **Secure Storage of Secrets:** Don't have them in plain text config files. Use Azure Key Vault or equivalents.
   - **Network Isolation:** Dev/test environments should be segmented from production, where possible.

4. **Continuous Monitoring**
   - **Intrusion Detection:** Monitor for suspicious activity in your production environment.
   - **Audit Logs:** Maintain clear records of who did what, where. Invaluable during security incident investigations.

Tools & Techniques for Azure DevOps

- **Azure Policy:** Enforce rules throughout your Azure subscriptions. Example: "Virtual Machines must run approved OS images."
- **Dependency Scanning:** Integrations with tools like OWASP Dependency Check or GitHub's built-in security features.
- **Static Code Analysis:** Many tools exist (SonarQube, Checkmarx, etc.) to detect insecure coding patterns alongside traditional linting.
- **Azure Pipelines Security Tasks:** There are marketplace extensions specifically designed to integrate security steps into your pipelines.

Example: Security Steps for our Game

1. **Pipeline Step:** Run a vulnerability scan on your container images as part of the build process.
2. **Azure Policies:** Prevent deployment of web apps that are publicly accessible without HTTPS enabled.
3. **Monitoring:** Configure alerts for anomalous login activity on your database (potential brute-force attack indicator).

Additional Resources

- **Microsoft Security Development Lifecycle (SDL):** https://www.microsoft.com/en-us/securityengineering/sdl
- **OWASP Top 10 (Web Application Vulnerabilities):** https://owasp.org/Top10/

Next Steps

Security is an ongoing journey. Next, we'll look at how Azure Cost Management can help you control expenditure as your usage of cloud services and infrastructure scales alongside your application's success.

Optimizing Infrastructure Costs with Azure Cost Management

Why Costs Matter in a DevOps World

- **Cloud Myth:** "The cloud is endlessly cheap." The reality is you pay for what you use, and those costs can scale unexpectedly.
- **Empowerment:** Developers, armed with cost data, can make better choices about resource sizing, architectural patterns, and tradeoffs between cost and performance.
- **Accountability:** DevOps means ownership over the whole lifecycle. That includes the financial impact of your technical decisions.

Azure Cost Management & Analysis

- **Centralized View:** Breaks down costs by subscription, resource group, service (e.g., "Azure App Service," "CosmosDB"), even down to individual resources.
- **Filtering & Granularity:** Slice data by timeframe, tags you've applied to resources, and more. "Show me the most expensive VMs over the last month."
- **Forecasting:** Projects future spending trends based on past usage, helping avoid budgetary surprises.
- **Budgets & Alerts:** Set spending limits, get notified before you exceed them.

Optimization Tactics

Let's look at practical cost-saving actions, often made possible by insights from Cost Management:

- **Right-Sizing Resources:** VMs that are consistently underutilized are prime candidates for downsizing, saving you hourly fees.
- **Utilize Reservations:** If you have predictable workloads, committing to 1-year or 3-year Azure Reserved Instances offers significant discounts over pay-as-you-go.

- **Autoscaling:** Match infrastructure capacity to demand. Scale down during off-peak hours when possible.
- **Dev/Test on a Schedule:** Non-production environments might only need to run during work hours. Power them down automatically for nights and weekends.
- **Efficient Storage:** Archive old data to cheaper storage tiers. Azure Blob Storage offers "hot," "cool," and "archive" access tiers with varying price points.

Example: Putting your Quiz Game on a Diet

1. **Analyze in Cost Management:** Is your database over-provisioned? Are there unused VMs leftover from a past experiment?
2. **Set a Budget:** Establish a target, and get an alert if you're trending towards exceeding it.
3. **Right-size:** During low-traffic periods, consider a lower database performance tier, or use built-in autoscaling features to dynamically adjust resources.

Additional Resources

- **Azure Cost Management Documentation:** https://docs.microsoft.com/en-us/azure/cost-management/
- **Azure Pricing Calculator:** Get estimates before provisioning resources https://azure.microsoft.com/en-us/pricing/calculator/

Next Steps

Optimization is an ongoing process. Next, we'll discuss how to cultivate a culture of continuous improvement where feedback loops drive both your applications and your DevOps practices to ever-greater success.

Continuous Improvement: Implementing Feedback Loops and Iterative Development

The Old Way vs. The DevOps Way

- **Old Way:** Long development cycles, infrequent releases, feedback came *after* a major version was already in the hands of users. This made it slow to course-correct.
- **DevOps Way:** Small iterations, frequent deployments, monitoring how real users interact with your system, and the ability to react quickly.

Types of Feedback Loops

1. **User Feedback:**
   - **In-App Surveys:** Quick pulse-checks on new features.
   - **Support Tickets:** Analyze common complaints, point to areas needing refinement.
   - **Social Media:** Monitor what people are saying organically – it might reveal unexpected use cases or frustrations.
2. **Monitoring & Telemetry:**
   - **Success Rates:** Are features being *actually* used? A fancy new report that nobody needs is a sign of misaligned effort.
   - **Errors:** Even if not reported by users, your logs will reveal pain points to address for a smoother experience.
3. **Internal Team Feedback:**
   - **Retrospectives:** Dedicated sessions within your team to analyze "what went well?" and "what could be better?" This extends to your DevOps process itself.
   - **Deployment Pain Points:** If deployments are consistently a headache, that's a feedback loop telling you to invest in improving your pipelines.
4. **Business/Market Feedback:**
   - **Competitor Analysis:** Are new rivals popping up with compelling features?

- ○ **Sales Trends:** If a major selling point is rarely utilized, it might be a candidate for rethinking or better onboarding of those customers.

Iterative Development

This is how you ACTION feedback:

- **Prioritize Relentlessly:** You can't fix everything at once. Focus on changes with the highest impact, whether that's delighting users or unblocking your team's own efficiency.
- **Small Batches:** Avoid monolithic releases. Each change is easier to test, roll out safely, and measure the impact.
- **Embrace Experimentation:** Canary releases, A/B testing… try new features with a subset of users to gather data before rolling them out widely.

Example: Evolving your Quiz Game

1. **Metrics Show:** A drop-off in usage of a recently released leaderboard feature.
2. **User Survey:** Reveals many players find it confusing and difficult to understand.
3. **Iterate:** Simplify the leaderboard design, roll it out gradually.
4. **Observe:** Do usage and overall positive sentiment increase?

Additional Resources

- **The Lean Startup (Book):** Popularized the "build-measure-learn" loop, highly relevant to DevOps https://theleanstartup.com/
- **Etsy's Blog on Experimentation:** Great examples of a tech company doing this at scale https://codeascraft.com/

Next Steps

A culture of continuous improvement is self-reinforcing. Now let's explore how to adapt your DevOps practices as your team, projects, and user base grow.

Scaling Your DevOps Practices: Strategies for Growth and Expansion

Common Growing Pains

- **Pipelines Get Unwieldy:** As complexity increases, build and release pipelines become a maze of tasks and dependencies.
- **Knowledge Silos:** Early on, everyone might know how everything works. This breaks down in larger teams, leading to bottlenecks and confusion during incidents.
- **Inconsistent Environments:** The dreaded "it works on my machine" syndrome becomes more frequent, hindering the reliability of your process.
- **Security as an Afterthought:** When moving fast in the beginning, it's tempting to delay rigorous security. This becomes a major risk as you scale.

Scaling Teams & Collaboration

- **Break Down Monoliths:** If feasible, decompose large applications into smaller services with clearer ownership boundaries. This allows teams to iterate more independently.
- **InnerSource:** Encourage a culture within your organization of treating even internal projects with the rigor of open-source – good documentation, contribution guidelines, etc.
- **Cross-Team Scrums:** Representatives from each team syncing up regularly improves visibility and helps resolve dependencies early.

Scaling Infrastructure

- **Infrastructure as Code (IaC):** Tools like ARM Templates (Azure) or Terraform make provisioning environments repeatable and versionable. This is crucial in multi-environment scenarios.
- **Embrace the Cloud Fully:** Autoscaling, serverless functions… these help your infrastructure adapt to unpredictable demand, and potentially reduce costs.

- **Templatize Pipelines:** Shareable pipeline fragments reduce redundancy and promote consistency.

Scaling Processes

- **Formalize Change Management:** It's not about slowing things down with bureaucracy, but ensuring large changes are well-communicated and risk is assessed.
- **Documentation is Your Friend:** Not thrilling, but knowledge bases, runbooks, and clear onboarding materials are essential as your team grows.
- **Automate the Toil:** If you are doing a repetitive task manually, chances are high that it can be automated, freeing your team's time for higher-value work.

Example: Scaling Up your Quiz Game

1. **Microservices?:** Break out the leaderboard system, maybe payment processing… allowing those components to be owned by dedicated teams.
2. **IaC for Environments:** Ensure your staging environment truly mirrors production to avoid surprises during "big" deployments.
3. **Security Gates:** Automated checks in your build pipelines fail builds if vulnerabilities or outdated library dependencies are detected.

Additional Resources

- **Team Topologies (Book):** Patterns for organizing tech teams in a rapidly changing environment https://teamtopologies.com/
- **Azure Well-Architected Framework:** Provides guidance, including aspects highly relevant to scaling https://docs.microsoft.com/azure/architecture/framework/

Continuous Improvement Applies to DevOps Itself

Scaling is an ongoing journey! Remember those feedback loops:

- **Monitor Your CI/CD:** How long do builds take? How frequently do deployments fail? Look for these metrics as leading indicators of friction in your process.
- **Developer Experience Surveys:** Keep a pulse on your team's own satisfaction with your tooling and processes. This reveals bottlenecks much faster before they affect your product's delivery.

Conclusion

Throughout this book, you've gained a comprehensive understanding of Azure DevOps and the transformative power it brings to software development. Let's recap some of the highlights:

- **The Why of DevOps** You've seen how it breaks down silos between development and operations, leading to faster delivery, higher-quality applications, and happier teams.
- **Azure DevOps as Your Toolkit:** You've mastered the fundamentals of Azure Boards for agile planning, Azure Repos for code collaboration, and Azure Pipelines for automating builds, tests, and deployments.
- **Beyond the Basics:** You delved into the world of continuous monitoring, applying tools like Application Insights and Log Analytics to proactively maintain your applications' health.
- **DevSecOps:** We emphasized the importance of embedding security at every stage of your pipeline, not just as an afterthought.
- **Optimization is Ongoing:** You learned how to use Azure Cost Management to keep your cloud expenses in check, and how feedback loops drive continuous improvement within your development practices.

The Journey Continues

Implementing DevOps isn't a one-time project; it's an evolving mindset. Remember these principles as you continue your journey:

- **Embrace Automation:** Eliminate manual and error-prone processes wherever possible. Your pipelines are your most powerful assets.
- **Data is Your Guide:** Metrics from monitoring, insights from cost analysis, and continuous feedback will illuminate the best path forward.
- **Experiment and Iterate:** Don't be afraid to try new tools, refine your processes, and adapt as your projects and team evolve.

- **Community Matters:** The DevOps ecosystem is vast and supportive. Tap into the shared knowledge and learn from others' experiences.

Your Transformation Starts Here

Whether you're a seasoned developer, a project manager new to the technical side, or anyone looking to streamline their software development processes, this book has equipped you with the foundation to excel.

With Azure DevOps as your ally, you're ready to confidently build, test, and deploy amazing applications. The world is waiting for what you'll create next!